THE CHEAP BASTARD'S® GUIDE TO

Houston

HELP US KEEP THIS GUIDE UP TO DATE

We would love to hear from you concerning your experiences with this guide and how you feel it could be improved and kept up to date. Please send your comments and suggestions to:

editorial@globepequot.com

Thanks for your input, and happy travels!

CHEAP BASTARD'S® SERIES

THE CHEAP BASTARD'S® GUIDE TO

Houston

Secrets of Living the Good Life—**For Less!**

First Edition

Kristin **Finan**

gpp®
travel

Guilford, Connecticut
An imprint of Globe Pequot Press

All the information in this guidebook is subject to change. We recommend that you call ahead to obtain current information before traveling.

To buy books in quantity for corporate use
or incentives, call **(800) 962–0973**
or e-mail **premiums@GlobePequot.com**.

Cheap Bastard's Guide is a registered trademark of Rob Grader.

Text design by Sheryl P. Kober

Library of Congress Cataloging-in-Publication Data is available on file.

ISBN: 978-0-7627-6456-3

Printed in the United States of America
10 9 8 7 6 5 4 3 2 1

For Kona Isabelle,
evidence that the best things in life are indeed free.

CONTENTS

SECTION 3: Exploring Houston

Appendices

ABOUT THE AUTHOR

Kristin Finan is a writer, author, and enthusiastic *frugalista* living in Houston. This is her second book; her first book, *Quick Escapes from Houston* (Globe Pequot Press), was released in late 2010. Her work regularly appears in the *Houston Chronicle,* one of the largest daily newspapers in the country, as well as other national publications. She is a proud graduate of the University of Texas at Austin and thinks the only thing Houston is lacking is a Krispy Kreme. She can be contacted at www.kristinfinan.com.

ACKNOWLEDGMENTS

Throughout my research I was surrounded by people who unselfishly channeled their own inner cheap bastards to make recommendations for this book. I wish I could pay each of you with the money you saved me, but that wouldn't be a wise financial investment, so I'll just offer a warm and heartfelt thank you instead. I couldn't have done it without you. Here are a few people I'd like to thank in particular.

First, the biggest thank you to my daughter, Kona, and my husband, Patrick, who acted as playground testers, free pizza tasters, and Astros seat fillers throughout this journey. Your endless patience, insight, and encouragement are unparalleled. I love you.

Thanks also to my mom and dad, Jeanne and George, for making me the *frugalista* I am today. Any success I have I owe to you.

Also, much appreciation to my friends and family who ventured out with me in the name of research (and happy hour) or tossed great ideas my way, particularly Benjamin Finan, Cookie Roberts, Monica Haas, Rachel Gale, Keri Wiginton, Gina Finan, Brittney Mitchell, Tammy Portnoy, K. J. Joshi, Amora Rodrigues, Pat Cowherd, Maritza Antu, Camille Truong, and Andrea Youck. Thanks also to Lindsey Brown with the Greater Houston Convention and Visitors Bureau, who provided me with a wealth of ideas.

Finally, thanks to Kevin Sirois, Amy Lyons, and the rest of the gang at Globe Pequot Press for the opportunity and support.

INTRODUCTION

As the youngest of four, I find that most of my childhood vacation memories stem from trekking around the country in a loaded Volvo station wagon with a luggage carrier up top. When we stopped for the night, we usually camped, stayed with relatives, or spent the night at Motel 6. It wasn't that we couldn't have stayed elsewhere; it was just that my dad really liked getting a good deal.

When I was thirteen I got my first lesson about the benefits of spending money wisely. As part of a class project about the stock market, we were told to pick companies to invest in—whoever made the most imaginary money would score a $50 gift card for Circle K. Thanks to a few tips from my parents, I won the contest, spent the $50 on a couple of cases of Snickers, and had a revelation: Investing wisely was *cool*.

Since then, I've tried to be careful about how I spend my money. When I got married, I countered our decision to have an open bar by wearing a $200 dress (don't worry—it was fabulous). It's not that I'm cheap (all the time, at least); it's just that I pay attention to where my money is going and try to make sure I'm being smart about it.

That said, you won't see in this book suggestions such as eat at Taco Bell, cut your own hair, or run outside instead of getting a gym membership. A "Cheap Bastard" is not a stingy person, but rather a proud term used to describe someone who loves the thrill of saving a buck or two.

I believe you can do all the finest things in life—wine, dinner, dancing, theater—in a frugal way by doing your research ahead of time. It's amazing what a little effort will get you.

That's what this book is about. I've done the digging in Houston, my home, so you can save a buck. The great thing about a major city like Houston is that it is absolutely filled with wonderful finds.

The fourth largest city in the country, this place has it all: a world-class arts scene, major sports teams, incredible restaurants, fantastic museums. And because we lack the pomp and circumstance you may find in other cities, you'll see more opportunities here to get a deal.

Want to see a Broadway show? The Cheap Bastard can get you in for free. Dying to try the famous dishes at t'afia restaurant? Don't pay—the Cheap Bastard will tell you how to get them on the house. Always wanted to try a yoga class? The Cheap Bastard has your free admission. No matter what you want to try in this city, there's a way to save as you're doing it. And it's all perfectly legal.

This book includes a variety of listings intended to direct you to the best deals. The first are free listings, meaning the event, activity, or place is free. Some are free all the time, while others are free but have restrictions. Whenever a place is only free part of the time or requires something additional from you in order to receive the free admission, the entry will include a line that says *The Catch*.

The other type of listing included in this book is cheap deals, meaning that you have to pay for them but that they are still a great price. Some are always discounted, while others offer deals on particular days and times.

This book is intended for both locals and visitors interested in getting the most for their money, from foreign businessmen and women in town for work, to young professionals, to families raising their little ones here. There's no reason that you shouldn't get your money's worth each and every time you go out.

Everything in this guide is accurate as of press time, but as things frequently change, you may want to call ahead or go online to check before you go.

SECTION 1:

Entertainment in Houston

THEATER:
IN ON THE ACT

"If it's a good script I'll do it. And if it's a bad script, and they pay me enough, I'll do it."

—GEORGE BURNS

If there is one thing Houstonians are proud of, it's their art scene. It's a standout across the board, but the live performance element of it is particularly robust. If you wanted to, you could see a different show every night of the week. And even better, tickets are usually affordable, if not free. What's offered here is a guide to the best places to see such shows.

But first, a note on scoring cheap tickets: If you're willing to do a little ushering, bartending, or hammering on the set, you're a valuable commodity to theater companies, particularly the smaller ones. Almost all of the companies listed are eager for volunteers and will let you watch the show (or even give you free tickets to other shows) if you sign up to help out.

Not into volunteering? Another great option is attending previews to upcoming performances, when tickets are generally deeply discounted. I've listed the theaters that offer preview performances below.

ALWAYS **FREE**

This theater always offers fabulous free shows to the general public.

Miller Outdoor Theatre
6000 Hermann Park Dr.
(281) 823-9103
www.milleroutdoortheatre.com

Street Beat
Hamlet
~~A Midsummer Night's Dream~~
Comedy of Errors

If you've heard about Miller Outdoor Theatre but never really understood what it's all about, here's the deal. Located in Houston's popular Hermann Park, this outdoor theater has seats for 1,700 people (the adjacent lawn can accommodate 4,500 more—just bring a blanket to sit on) who want to attend their free shows, offered eight months out of the year. But this isn't some thrown together production. These are professional entertainers putting on shows you could just as easily see at a major theater, such as *Disney's Beauty and the Beast*, *42nd Street*, and *South Pacific*. The largest free program of its kind in the nation, it offers everything from Shakespeare to ballet to films at this gorgeous facility; shows are always family friendly. Some shows require tickets for the covered seating area. Check the website for upcoming performances and policies.

MAJOR **SHOWS,** MAJOR **DEALS**

Here's how to score a free or cheap seat at Houston's biggest performances.

Alley Theatre
615 Texas St.
(713) 220-5700
www.alleytheatre.org

Book soon. Agatha Christie!

Seeing a show at the Alley Theatre is an absolute must if you're living in—or even just visiting—Houston. This major company puts on a variety of performances every year with a mission of offering everything from well-known plays to new, rarely performed, and newly rediscovered work. The emphasis here is to touch audiences and make them think about things they've never considered before while thoroughly supporting a company of actors, designers, artisans, and craftspeople year-round. The theater has two stages: the 824-seat Hubbard Stage and the 310-seat Neuhaus Stage. No matter what you see on your visit here, chances are good you're going to love it. Ticket prices can vary greatly depending on the show. "Cheap Thrills" tickets, which are available for Sunday and Tuesday evening performances, start at $21, a steal compared to the usual ticket prices. Check the website for more details.

~~Ballet Barre~~
The Wortham Center, 501 Texas St.
(713) 522-5538
www.houstonballet.org/balletbarre

If you're under forty and appreciate the ballet (or think you might appreciate it, given proper exposure), you can't miss out on Ballet Barre, the Houston Ballet's group for young professionals. When you join, you get tickets to four performances as well as invitations to social and networking events, elite access to the Masterson Green Room during intermission, and discounts to the Houston Ballet Ball and Nutcracker Market Preview Party. Free booze is also frequently included. Membership starts at $125—a great deal considering that a ticket in the same seating area for a single show can run you $88 or higher.

The Hobby Center for the Performing Arts
800 Bagby St.
(713) 315-2400
www.thehobbycenter.org

Rhythm of the Night

This sprawling, beautifully designed theater brings in all kinds of shows, from concerts to dance performances to opera to touring Broadway acts. Recent shows here have included Adam Lambert, Amy Grant, *Shrek the Musical,* and *Hairspray.* Unfortunately, because of the high caliber of the shows that come through here, ticket prices can be expensive. However, if you're willing to volunteer, you can see these shows for free!

Jones Hall for the Performing Arts
615 Louisiana St.
(713) 227-3974
www.houstontx.gov/joneshall

This facility is best known as home to the Houston Symphony (www.houston symphony.org), but it also hosts other groups and performances throughout the year. If you're interested in seeing the symphony, you're in good company: The hall can seat more than 2,000 people with every performance. And if you're looking for a good deal, you're in luck, because the symphony offers a variety of discounts to theatergoers. If you're a student, you're eligible for rush tickets, meaning that if you show up for a show an hour and a half early and there are still seats open, you can score a ticket for just $12. Rush tickets for senior citizens are $15. Young professionals under forty are also eligible for discounted tickets.

Wortham Theatre Center
500 Texas St.
(713) 237-1439
www.houstontx.gov/worthamcenter

Romeo & Juliet

Home to both the Houston Ballet (www.houstonballet.org) and the Houston Grand Opera (www.houstongrandopera.org), this 430,000-square-foot facility features two theaters that also host smaller performances and concerts by groups such as the Society for the Performing Arts (www.spahouston.org) and Da Camera of Houston (www.dacamera.com) throughout the year. You'll want to check with the individual organizations for ticketing, but discounts for students, seniors, young professionals, and volunteers are typically available. If you're under twenty-five, you can get a $15 ticket (or two tickets for $25) for Friday evening performances. There is also a young professionals program that includes discount tickets for people under forty.

X SMALL **THEATERS,** BIG **SAVINGS**

The Company OnStage
536 Westbury Sq.
(713) 726-1219
www.companyonstage.org

This nonprofit theater company prides itself on offering professional, high-quality contemporary and classic shows for children and adults in a welcoming, intimate arena. Putting on about a half dozen shows a year with both its evening and children's theater programs, the Company OnStage offers lots of opportunities to see a great, affordable show. Most evening tickets are around $15 ($13 for seniors and students); shows are held at 8 p.m. on Fri and Sat. Children's shows are held at 11 a.m. and 1:30 p.m. on Sat and are $8. Coupon books and other discounts are available online. Reservations are recommended. Theater classes are also offered periodically; check the website for details. Here's a tip: Volunteer here and see shows for free!

X Crighton Theatre
234 Main St., Conroe
(936) 441-7469
www.crightontheatre.org

You'll have to drive to get there, but this theater on the main drag in Conroe is worth the trip thanks to its solid regular lineup of performances. As the base for companies such as Stage-Right Productions, the Montgomery County Performing Arts Society, and The Sounds of Texas Music Series, the theater offers great shows here throughout the year. One of the benefits of its location out of the main Houston arts district is that the theater can offer shows at a lower price, with some children's productions going for as low as $5 each.

Dress to Impress

We may not be Dallas, but when it comes to gussying up for a special event, we Houstonians can clean up with the best of them. If you've got tickets for the ballet, theater, symphony, or other performing arts event, here's a guide to how to dress. As a general rule, though, it's better to be overdressed than underdressed.

For the Alley: Outfits vary, but for evening shows most people dress as they would if they were going out for a nice dinner or heading to church.

For the Houston Ballet: The ballet recommends wearing business casual clothing (or more formal attire) to its performances, as the audience tends to dress up. Also, bring a wrap or jacket, as the theater can get cold, particularly if you have tickets in the orchestra section.

For a show at the Hobby Center: According to the center, visitors should be appropriate but comfortable. Think business casual attire or cocktail dresses and suits. And bring a wrap or a jacket so you'll stay comfortable in the air-conditioning.

For the Houston Symphony: The symphony reports a range of dress, from formal attire down. To be safe, go with business casual (or something even more formal). You can't be too dressy here.

For the Miller Outdoor Theater: Dress comfortably. You're going to be outside, so staying cool is going to be key here. Shorts and sandals are perfectly fine.

For a performance at one of the smaller theaters: Dress as you would to a nice dinner or show. For women, think slacks, a cute dress, or a skirt and blouse. For guys, think khakis and a button-up shirt.

For a comedy club: Jeans and a button-up shirt are fine. Dress in what you'd wear on a casual date.

Ensemble Theater
3535 Main St.
(713) 520-0055
www.ensemblehouston.com

The oldest and largest professional African-American theater in the Southwest, the Ensemble has become a Houston institution thanks to its high-quality, affordable shows. The mission here is to draw a multicultural audience from all walks of life, and with recent performances such as *The Waiting Room, Cinderella, Gee's Bend,* and *Jitney,* the theater is doing just that. To get a good deal here, attend a preview performance of an opening show, when tickets are just $12 for nonmusicals (regularly $35 on opening night) and $20 for musicals (regularly $45 on opening night). Matinee and Thursday evening discounts are also available.

Main Street Theater Company
2540 Times Blvd.
(713) 524-6706
www.mainstreettheater.com

Located in the bustling Rice Village area, Main Street Theater Company is used to entertaining a sophisticated, demanding audience. And the company always delivers. Formed in the 1970s, Main Street now operates two theaters that produce large-scale classics and musicals as well as hosting a youth theater program. Recent performances have included *The Doctor's Dilemma, The Heidi Chronicles, A Catered Affair,* and *The Year of Magical Thinking.* The company also offers Kids On Stage, family-friendly performances put on by children for just $5. Regular show tickets are $26 for Thursday and Friday performances, $30 for opening night and Saturday and Sunday performances. Student tickets and tickets for preview performances are $10. A second theater is located at 4617 Montrose Blvd. (713-524-6706).

O'Kane Theatre
1 Main St., at the University of Houston Downtown
(713) 221-8104
www.uhd.edu

Part of the Department of Arts and Humanities at the University of Houston Downtown, the O'Kane Theatre has been putting on shows for the past thirty-five years, ranging from *Ain't Misbehavin'* to *Romeo and Juliet* to *A*

Few Good Men. The shows are typically under $10 (sometimes free) and open to the public. Because the theater is small, it gives visitors an intimate, up-close feel for the performances. Touring shows also sometimes perform here. Check the website for shows and schedules.

Pasadena Little Theatre
4318 Allen Genoa Rd., Pasadena
(713) 941-1758
www.pasadenalittletheatre.org

This great little theater company offers a variety of shows throughout the year, such as *The Wizard of Oz, Born Yesterday,* and *Damn Yankees.* It may not be the most upscale place you've ever been, but the performances are fun and always affordable. Reservations are recommended; tickets are usually around $14 for adults and $12 for students and seniors. If you get a season pass, you'll save about 30 percent off the regular price of shows. Volunteers, cast, and crew are also always needed.

Stages Repertory Theatre
3201 Allen Parkway, Suite 101
(713) 527-0220
www.stagestheatre.com

Formed in the damp basement of a brewery in 1978, this now well-known theater company puts on some of the greatest plays in the city, blending talented casts and a penchant for taking a unique approach to classic plays to make them their own. The productions here often take risks, and it works. You won't soon forget a show you see here. MainStage productions are typically for mature audiences only and are held at 7:30 p.m. on Wed and Thurs, 8 p.m. on Fri, 3 and 8 p.m. on Sat, and 3 p.m. on Sun; tickets typically start around $17. There is also an EarlyStages program for children with performances held several times a year. Tickets usually cost around $9; contact the theater for details. Volunteer with Stages to receive free tickets to performances.

Texas Repertory Theatre
14243 Stuebner Airline Rd.
(281) 583-7573
www.texreptheatre.org

It may have its hub in northwest Houston, but this theater company draws visitors from around the city for its great productions of plays such as *A Flea in Her Ear, Miracle on 34th Street,* and *Little Shop of Horrors.* Performances typically cost around $25, but discounts are available for seniors, military personnel, and students (a valid student ID will get you 50 percent off performances). If you're willing to volunteer, you can trade your time for a free show. Youth classes are also available.

Theatre Southwest
8944-A Clarkcrest St.
(713) 661-9505
www.theatresouthwest.org

Theatre Southwest has been presenting performances since 1957 and now offers a six-play season that draws audiences from around Houston every year. In addition to shows, the theater offers monthly meetings and workshops the third Wednesday of every month. Tickets are $16 for adults, $14 for seniors sixty-five and up, and $14 for students with valid ID; group discounts are also available.

Theatre Suburbia
4106 Way Out West Dr.
(713) 682-3525
www.theatresuburbia.org

Northwest Houston's longest running volunteer playhouse, Theatre Suburbia is like the little theater that could, turning out 341 shows to date and celebrating its forty-ninth season this year. The theater typically offers seven shows a year, with performances running for five weeks on Friday and Saturday, with a few Sunday matinees thrown in for good measure. Recent performances have included *Only an Orphan Girl, The Philadelphia Story,* and *A Good Old Fashioned Redneck Country Christmas.* Tickets cost $14 for adults and $13 for students and seniors for the 8:30 shows on Fri and Sat, and $12 for the 3 p.m. matinee on Sun. Season tickets are also available, and volunteers are welcome. Theatre Suburbia offers free preview performances on the Thurs before a show opens to the public. No reservations are required.

MUSIC:
GETTING IN TUNE

*"I'd rather be dead than singing
'Satisfaction' when I'm forty-five."*

—MICK JAGGER

Austin, the "live music capital of the world," steals the spotlight a lot when it comes to music. Sure, it's got Austin City Limits, the SXSW festival, and a lot of hipster street cred. But a little-known fact about Houston is that we get almost all of the same bands coming through that Austin does. And because Houston isn't quite so in your face about it, cover charges can be significantly cheaper. Here's a rundown of the city's best music venues.

BIG **ACT,** BIG **DEAL**

Houston has several major concert venues that regularly draw the world's biggest touring artists. It can be harder to get a good deal at these places (when you're drawing crowds of thousands, what's the incentive?). Still, sometimes you can find bargains. Here are some of the best options.

Cynthia Woods Mitchell Pavilion
2005 Lake Robbins Dr., The Woodlands
(281) 363-3300
www.woodlandscenter.org

This open-air concert venue is probably my favorite place to see a show in Houston. First off, it draws major national acts, from John Mayer to Paramore to Counting Crows to the Jonas Brothers. Second, in addition to reserved seating in front of the stage, there's also seating up on the hill, where tickets are cheaper and you can spread out a blanket and watch the show under the stars. The venue also hosts symphony and children's events. General admission lawn tickets for major acts typically start around $30, with discounts if you buy four tickets or more. Or you can volunteer and see the shows for free.

Grand 1894 Opera House
2020 Post Office St., Galveston
(409) 763-7173
www.thegrand.com

OK, so you'll have to drive the hour to Galveston, but no Houstonian should miss the chance to visit this historic and majestic venue, which has survived hurricane after hurricane to bring some of the best touring concerts, plays, and comedians to the area. Tickets typically start around $20, but if you're willing to volunteer, you can see the shows for free.

● House of Blues
1204 Caroline St.
(713) 652-5837
www.houseofblues.com

With recent acts such as Talib Kweli, Margaret Cho, and Michael Franti, relative newcomer House of Blues Houston is making a name for itself as a go-to concert venue. General admission tickets start around $20; discounts are available if you buy a four-pack of tickets. Shows are all ages. Show a dinner or store receipt from the House of Blues the night of your show and receive priority entrance into the music hall.

Not feeling like an evening show? Try the famous Gospel Brunch, where, for less than $40, you can get a fantastic gospel show and an amazing brunch with items such as spinach and artichoke frittata, red beans and rice, pesto chicken pasta, and biscuits and gravy. Seating is at noon on Sun.

Toyota Center
1510 Polk St.
(713) 758-7200
www.houstontoyotacenter.com

Home base for the Houston Rockets, the Toyota Center is also one of Houston's most notable concert venues, hosting everyone from Bruce Springsteen to Lady Gaga to Justin Timberlake. It's a huge, stadium-type venue, but if you want to see the biggest artists, this is frequently your only choice. The good news is that thanks to its size, the range of ticket prices varies greatly, starting as low as $20 for big-name acts. Still too expensive for you? You can always try your luck on a discount ticket site such as www.stubhub.com, which frequently has good deals.

Verizon Wireless Amphitheater
520 Texas St.
(713) 230-1666
www.verizonwirelesstheatre.com

Judging by the name of this place, you may come in expecting to find a giant venue, but with a capacity of less than 3,000, it's actually a rather intimate place to see a show. Recent concerts here have included Ryan Adams, Vampire Weekend, the Pixies, and Megadeth. Tickets start around $30.

Warehouse Live
813 Saint Emanuel St.
(713) 225-5483
www.warehouselive.com

Located adjacent to the downtown corridor, this repurposed 1920s-era building hosts some of the best smaller concerts in town. An independent venue that can accommodate up to 1,500, this is a great place to see up-and-coming touring acts right before they hit it big. Recent concerts here have included the Kottonmouth Kings, Bad Religion, Ghostland Observatory, and Dr. Dog. Most shows are all ages. If you're twenty-one and up, show up an hour early and receive happy hour prices at the bar. You can also join the Warehouse Live street team and get free tickets that way.

Rock Out at the Rodeo

Every February and March, the greatest performers in the world flood Houston's Reliant Park complex for a little event called the **Houston Livestock Show and Rodeo.** Every year it brings in a range of performers, from Hannah Montana to George Strait. If you want in on a piece of the action, you have to keep an eye out for when the lineup is announced, typically in the fall. Performances begin at 6:45 p.m. on weekdays and at 3:45 p.m. on weekends. All performances begin with rodeo action and are followed by the show. Upper level tickets start at $18 and include both the rodeo and concert, not a bad deal considering the average price of concert tickets these days. For information visit www.rodeohouston.com.

Want to avoid high ticket prices for concerts? Take in a show at the **Hideout,** a tent located on rodeo grounds with live music, drinks, and dancing. Just buy a general admission ticket to the rodeo for $7 and get into the Hideout for free. Open nightly for those twenty-one and up during rodeo season.

SMALLER **VENUES**

Anderson Fair
2007 Grant St.
(832) 212-4057
www.andersonfair.com

This is one of the more underground concert venues in Houston, which means you can see great Texas artists for much lower ticket prices, typically between $10 and $15. Doors open at 8 p.m. for shows. Wine by the glass or bottle is available, as is domestic and imported beer and nonalcoholic drinks. Food includes "killer nachos," chicken and spinach quesadillas, stuffed potatoes, chips and salsa, and popcorn.

Big Easy Social & Pleasure Club
5731 Kirby Dr.
(713) 523-9999
www.thebigeasyblues.com

The name may sound like something off a strip club, but this is actually one of the best places to check out live blues in town. With local bands playing blues six nights a week (Sunday nights are reserved for zydeco music), you're pretty certain to hear something good no matter when you go. Open 8 p.m. to 2 a.m. There's no cover Sun through Thurs and a $5 cover Fri through Sat. There's free pool on Mon, and a Domino's Pizza located right next door, should you get hungry.

Blanco's
3406 W. Alabama St.
(713) 439-0072
www.houstonredneck.com/blancos.html

It's less well known than some of the other dance halls in town, but Blanco's is without question one of the best places to spank the planks with a backdrop of live country music. Bands play on Thurs and Fri starting at 9 p.m. Recent bands have included the Honky Tonk Heroes, Miss Leslie and Her Juke-Jointers, and Bucko Ruckus. With band names like that, you can pretty much count on having a boot-stomping good time. Avoid paying a cover charge by going during happy hour, which runs from 11 a.m. to 9 p.m., and then staying for the band.

Cezanne
4100 Montrose Blvd.
(713) 522-9621
www.blacklabradorpub.com

Located over the Black Labrador Pub, this authentic jazz venue impresses visitors with its high-quality acoustic music in a comfortable atmosphere. One of the few places to find jazz in Houston, Cezanne is well worth the $10 cover.

Continental Club
3700 Main St.
(713) 529-9899
www.continentalclub.com

This offshoot of the popular Austin concert venue is a heavy hitter in its own right in Houston thanks to the variety and quality of the bands it brings in, from touring artists such as Wanda Jackson to local cover bands such as Beetle (they cover the Beatles—go figure) to dance-themed nights such as tango Mondays (lessons start at 7 p.m., and the band starts at 8 p.m.). The club also has a solid bar, outside patio, and cool bartenders. The Continental Club's sister bar, The Big Top (3714 Main St.), frequently offers live music with no cover.

Dan Electro's Guitar Bar
1031 E. 24th St.
(713) 862-8707
www.danelectrosguitarbar.com

The mix of artists here can be astounding, from old dudes jamming for the hell of it to belly dancing troupes to serious touring acts out to make a buck. That's the beauty of this place, where the motto is "absolutely alive music." Many shows are free, and if there is a cover it's generally $10 or under.

Dosey Doe Coffee House
25911 I-45 North, The Woodlands
(281) 367-3774
www.doseydoe.com

It calls itself a coffeehouse, but Dosey Doe is also becoming one of the premier venues for live Texas music in the area. Located inside a 150-year-old bar from Kentucky made from oak and birch, this restaurant and dance hall automatically gives you a laid-back southern vibe. The amazing artists who have performed there, such as Marcia Ball, Radney Foster, Tish Hinojosa, and Gary P. Nunn, add to the feel. Tickets start as low as $10 for some shows and go up for bigger acts. Feeling hungry? Don't miss the chicken-fried steak, washed down with something from the full bar.

Firehouse Saloon
5930 Southwest Freeway
(713) 977-1962
www.firehousesaloon.com

A hotbed for local and touring alt-country musicians, this is a really fun joint for a night out with friends. Toss on your cowboy boots, grab a shot of whiskey, and get yourself up front near the stage. Recent acts have included Jason Boland, Brandon Rhyder, and Bleu Edmonson. Shows are for those twenty-one and up and most cost around $10, although some are free. Firehouse Saloon is open from 4 p.m. to 2 a.m. Thurs through Sat. Shows start at 9:15 p.m., with the headliner starting at 11:15 p.m. unless otherwise noted. Happy hour is from 5 to 7 p.m. daily and features $2.50 domestic bottles.

Fitzgerald's
2706 White Oak Dr.
(713) 862-3838
www.fitzlive.com

Another great Houston concert venue, this Heights-area institution brings in a mix of bands, from better-known acts such as a Los Skarnales and Ethereal to tribute bands paying homage to the likes of Stevie Ray Vaughan and Janis Joplin. There's also a monthly "school of rock" featuring local bands. Doors typically open around 8 p.m. for shows; tickets are around $10.

Goode's Armadillo Palace
5015 Kirby Dr.
(713) 526-9700
www.thearmadillopalace.com

With delicious drinks, fantastic comfort food, and live music most nights of the week, this is a great place to go with friends for happy hour and stay for a concert. Part of the Goode Company restaurant chain, Armadillo Palace is the first to regularly draw and market live music. There's usually no cover here, and if there is a cover, it'll be only $5 or so.

Hickory Hollow
101 Heights Blvd.
(713) 869-6300
www.hickoryhollowrestaurant.com

By day, the Heights location of this barbecue joint is known for serving up succulent ribs, chicken, and brisket. By night, however, it draws crowds for its shows, held at 7 and 10 p.m. on Fri and 5:30 and 8:30 p.m. on Sat. Music ranges from bluegrass to country to swing, and there's never a cover. Check the website for upcoming bands.

Last Concert Cafe
1403 Nance St.
(713) 226-8563
www.lastconcert.com

This family-friendly Tex-Mex restaurant is also known for hosting live music every night of the week, from open mic night on Monday to a Wednesday pot roast to bigger shows on weekends. The cafe also offers lunch and a happy hour starting at 3 p.m. with $2 Shiner drafts and $3 house margaritas. Smaller shows are free; bigger shows require tickets. Check the website for details.

The Listening Room
508 Pecore St.
(713) 864-4260
www.listeningroomhouston.com

Featuring "concerts with a totally different vibe," this intimate venue aims to allow visitors to experience music in a new way by holding shows in a fitness studio. Seating is on the floor, and the format is laid back. Recent artists have included Sara Hickman, Terri Hendrix, Guy Forsyth, Malford Milligan, Monte Montgomery, and Loudon Wainwright III. Tickets vary depending on the artist but can start around $12. Visit the website to book tickets or for more information.

McGonigel's Mucky Duck

2425 Norfolk St.
(713) 528-5999
www.mcgonigels.com

One of Houston's favorite small concert venues, McGonigel's Mucky Duck features local singer-songwriters throughout the week, no cover "Irish sessions" on Wednesday, and touring acts such as Jack Saunders, Alex and Julie, and Somebody's Darling on weekends. The bar is also open for lunch Mon through Sat from 11 a.m., with food service continuing until 11 p.m. A "Sunday Supper Session" is held on weekends. Check the website for details.

Meridian

1503 Chartres St.
(713) 225-1717
www.meridianhouston.com

This concert spot brings in a wide mix of groups ranging from up-and-coming hip-hop artists to folk-rock superstars. Weekly events include a Monday night talent show (winner gets $75) and a Thursday Night Throwdown featuring local R & B artists, as well as touring shows throughout the week. Most shows are under $10.

Mr. Gino's Lounge

7306 Cullen Blvd.
(713) 738-0555

This blues joint is a dive in every sense of the word: The walls are decorated with family photos; the regulars all know each other; and you'd never find it unless you were looking for it. But if you do find it, you're in luck, because you've just stumbled upon one of the best places to hear live blues in Houston, anchored by live blues on Sun from 5 to 9 p.m. featuring I. J. Gosey and the Supremes. Sunday cover is $5 and includes music and free homemade food such as beef stew and potatoes. Only beer, wine, and mixers are served here, but customers are welcome to bring their own liquor.

Numbers Night Club

300 Westheimer Rd.
(713) 526-8338
www.numbersnightclub.com

On first impression, this place looks like something out of the film *Labyrinth*. It's dark, moody, and not particularly inviting. But once you get used to that, you'll be pleasantly surprised to learn that the mix of music played here makes it a lovely place to see a show. Touring acts include bands such as Atari Teenage Riot, Nevermore, and The Sleeping. Themed nights, including a local band showcase on Thurs and a fantastic '80s night with 50 cent draft beer and $1 wells on Fri, are also good times to visit.

Puffabelly's Old Depot
100 Main St., in Old Town Spring
(281) 350-3376

It's a bit of a trek to get there, but once you do, you'll be glad you made it. This restaurant offers fantastic country fare and live Texas music from artists such as Django Walker, Jason Allen, and Randy Brown throughout the week. Call for details.

Scout Bar
18307 Egret Bay Blvd.
(281) 335-0002
www.scoutbar.com

It's about twenty minutes from downtown Houston, but this cool music bar is definitely worth it. Bands play here every weekend, and weekly specials include $1.00 drinks and no cover on Wed; $2.00 "big ass" beer, $2.50 wells, and no cover on Thurs; and $5.00 pitchers, $2.50 Jager shots, and no cover on Sun. The bar also features a DJ on Thurs, Fri, and Sat starting around 10:30. The bar is open from 8 p.m. to 2 a.m. Wed through Sun.

Walter's on Washington
4215 Washington Ave.
(713) 862-2513
www.4215washington.com

Walter's was on uber-trendy Washington Avenue well before it was cool to be on Washington Avenue, and that's a pretty good metaphor for what you find when you come here: great, solid bands, just before they hit it big and just after. Recent tours have included The Shakes, My Milky Way Arms, and the Lower Dens. Most tickets are around $10, and performances are open to all ages unless noted.

Hailing from Houston

While you're researching this city's music scene, you should also know a little bit about the major acts that got their start here. Here are five artists who wouldn't have made it big if it wasn't for Houston.

Beyoncé

Probably the most obvious but also one of the best known, Ms. Knowles was born in Houston and got her start performing in various dancing and singing competitions around town when she was a child. She was even mentioned in the *Houston Chronicle* for her singing talent when she was just seven. In the early 1990s she became the integral part of the band Destiny's Child, and the rest is history.

ZZ Top

Does anyone rock harder than ZZ Top? Not in Houston. Formed in Houston in 1969, this hardworking band has been playing regularly ever since. They frequently include Texas references in their music, from the songs "La Grange" and "Rio Grande Mud" to the album *Tejas*. Guitarist Billy Gibbons is frequently seen in Houston, popping up as a special guest at area events.

Paul Wall

The rap scene in Houston has been important nationally for years now, and no rapper is a better ambassador for this city than Paul Wall. After partnering with fellow Houston rappers Chamillionaire and Mike Jones in his early days, Wall made a name for himself with his album *The People's Champ,* which debuted at No. 1 on the Billboard 200. He's continued to stay in the spotlight since.

Lyle Lovett

Born in the Houston suburb of Klein, Lyle Lovett was raised in Houston and attended Texas A & M University, rooming, interestingly, with Robert Earl Keen for part of this time. In 1986 he signed with MCA Records, and he has since won four Grammys. To the rest of the world, he may be best known for his two-year marriage to Julia Roberts, but to Texans, he'll always be one of the best singer-songwriters to come from these parts.

Blue October

Formed in Houston in 1995, this band made a name for itself winning over local fans for years before gaining major national attention with the song "Hate Me" in 2006. Since then, the band has toured the national talk show circuit and received heavy airplay across the country.

MUSIC & A MEAL

Heading out for dinner or to grab a drink? Why not enjoy some free live music while you're at it. Here are some places that regularly host free music for their customers.

Andalucia Tapas Restaurant and Bar
1201 San Jacinto St.
(832) 319-6673
www.andaluciatapas.com

If you're looking for authentic Spanish tapas, you'll want to try this relative newcomer to the scene, which features a huge selection of both hot and cold options. And if you're looking for authentic Spanish music, you won't go wrong here, either, with live flamenco dancing and music most weekend nights. Call for details and to make a reservation.

Bailey's American Grille
2320 Nasa Parkway, Seabrook
(281) 291-9100
www.baileysamericangrille.com

Who doesn't love brunch? If you come to Bailey's American Grille on a Sunday, you can expect to get a heaping helping of live jazz with your Bloody Mary. The menu includes items such as "Gulf Coast" fried green tomatoes, crab cakes Benedict, macadamia-crusted jumbo shrimp, and southern fried chicken and waffles, as well as bottomless mimosas. Menu items range from $12 to $30—much more affordable than some of the brunch buffets in town. Can't make brunch? Head to Bailey's on a Tuesday to try out half-price wine night.

Boom Boom Room
2518 Yale St.
(713) 868-3740
http://web.me.com/weshannon1/The_Boom_Room_Room/Home.html

This cool little spot is charming for several reasons, including its delectable panini menu and its eclectic decor. One of the best things about this spot, located in the historic Heights neighborhood, is its live music offered on Sat.

Call ahead for artists and information. The Boom Boom Room is open from 4 p.m. to 2 a.m. Tues through Sat.

Brian O'Neill's Irish Pub

5555 Morningside Dr.
(713) 522-2603
www.brianoneills.com

In addition to its great happy hour specials and decent food, Brian O'Neill's also offers live music on the patio throughout the week. Grab a cold pint, get a seat outside, and enjoy the atmosphere. The people-watching here is also fantastic.

The Bull & Bear Tavern and Eatery

11980 Westheimer Rd.
(281) 496-6655
www.thebullandbear-tavernandeatery.com

The motto is "where you meet your best friends," and after a karaoke night here, held on Friday nights, that might just be true. This friendly, welcoming spot is the kind of place where you come for a pint and stay for a night. Sure, karaoke isn't exactly live music, but since it's hosted by a DJ, it probably counts. Happy hour is held from 11 a.m. to 7 p.m. and includes discounts on wine, beer, and liquor. Karaoke starts at 9 p.m. Other weekly specials include half-price pizza and $4.99 hot wings, $3.00 domestic drafts, and $3.50 Guinness pints on Thurs. Monthly specials are also listed online. Open daily from 11 a.m. to 2 a.m.

Cellar 17

6608 FM 1960 Rd.
(281) 893-6400
www.cellar-17.com

This fun wine bar and boutique offers a variety of options for enjoying wine. Grab a glass off their extensive wine list, design your own flight, and sample a few or pick up a bottle to enjoy in the privacy of your home. My favorite way to enjoy their wine, however, is with live music, which is offered on Fri and Sat at 8 p.m.

The Chocolate Bar

2521 University Blvd.
(713) 520-8888
www.theoriginalchocolatebar.com

There are oh so many reasons to love this famous Houston sweet shop, which offers every type of dessert you can imagine, from chocolate pizza to the enormous Aunt Etta's chocolate cake to homemade ice cream in flavors such as chocolate banana pudding, orange sunrise, and brownie supreme. Even though you probably don't need any more reasons to go, here's another: live swing music at the University location on Thursday nights starting around 7 p.m. from Buzz and the Blue Cats Orchestra. You may even see dancers from the Houston Swing Dance Society showing off their moves. There's also music at their second location at 1835 W. Alabama St. (713-520-8599) on Tues.

Hugo's Mexican Restaurant

1600 Westheimer Rd.
(713) 524-7744
www.hugosrestaurant.net

This is one of the best restaurants in Houston, and on Sunday you can eat their delicious food to the sound to El Viento, their house band, which performs mariachi and Latin music on the balcony during brunch. Served from 10 a.m. to 2:30 p.m., Hugo's brunch is $27 for adults and $10 for children. Sounds like a lot, but for that price, you get a wide variety of fare including tamales, *mole verde,* quesadillas, ceviche, shrimp cocktail, and more.

Mo's . . . A Place for Steaks

1801 Post Oak Blvd.
(713) 877-0720
www.mosaplaceforsteaks.com

One of Houston's favorite places to see and be seen (everyone from Francis Ford Coppola to members of the Houston Texans have dined here), Mo's . . . A Place for Steaks draws people for both its amazing steaks and its amazing atmosphere. Contributing to that atmosphere is a baby grand piano, which is played nightly for the enjoyment of guests. Go during happy hour, order a discounted drink, and enjoy the music. If you go on a Thursday, you may not be able to hear it, however, thanks to the robust bar scene during happy hour, when the restaurant becomes a people-watching paradise.

Ouisie's Table
3939 San Felipe St.
(713) 528-2264
www.ouisiestable.com

This restaurant is becoming a popular venue for weddings because of its elegant but comfortable decor. But if you go for a meal and want to kick back to some tunes, you can do that, too. Jazz is offered Friday and Saturday nights during dinner, and a piano man plays during the restaurant's incredible Sunday brunch, which includes offerings such as sautéed belly of salmon with deviled eggs, crispy fried Gulf oysters, a bison burger, and grilled beef medallions and eggs. Dishes range from $10 to $25. The restaurant is open from 11 a.m. to 10 p.m. Mon through Thurs, 11 a.m. to 11 p.m. on Fri, 11 a.m. to 11 p.m. on Sat, and 10 a.m. to 10 p.m. on Sun.

Phil's Texas Barbecue
110 S. Heights Blvd.
(713) 862-8600
www.philstxbbq.com

This barbecue hot spot made a splash right from the start. Located along the Washington Corridor, the restaurant is big, bold, and bright, with lots of space and slow-cooked meats that will make your mouth water. The menu includes stuffed baked potatoes; barbecue platters with meats including sliced beef, jalapeño sausage, turkey, pork loin, ribs, and chicken; barbecue sandwiches; po'boys; charbroiled hamburgers; veggie platters; and desserts such as bananas Foster bread pudding, buttermilk pie, cobbler, and chocolate pecan pie. Now, they're stepping up their game even more with live music from local country and rock artists several times a month on Saturday evenings. Phil's is open from 11 a.m. to 10 p.m. Mon through Wed, 11 a.m. to 1 a.m. Thurs through Sat, and 11 a.m. to 10 p.m. on Sun. Karaoke is offered on Thursday nights.

Ray's Grill
8502 FM 359 Rd., Fulshear
(281) 533-0099

Featuring fare inspired by local farmers and ranchers, Ray's Grill is a breath of fresh air in the Houston restaurant scene. Ingredients are seasonal and local, with wide menu options. A $20 brunch is also offered on Sun; reservations are recommended. One of the best times to go to Ray's, however, is on jazz night on Thurs between 7 and 10 p.m. Complimentary wine tastings are also held on Thurs from 6 to 8 p.m. Other special events, such as cigar and scotch tastings and cooking classes, are held throughout the year. Happy hour is Tues through Sat from 5 to 7 p.m. The restaurant is open from 5 to 9:30 p.m. Tues through Thurs, 11 a.m. to 3 p.m. and 5 to 10 p.m. Fri through Sat, and 10:30 a.m. to 2 p.m. for Sunday brunch. Closed on Mon.

Red Cat Jazz Café
924 Congress St.
(713) 226-7870
www.redcatjazzcafe.com

How's this sound? Go out for a delicious Cajun dinner and get live jazz music to boot. That's what you get when you visit the Red Cat Jazz Café, which is located downtown and aims to create a French Quarter–like feel with its food and atmosphere. Menu items include Louisiana staples such as red beans and rice, crawfish étouffée, and po'boys, as well as standards such as Caesar salad, French fries, and pork chops. Shows are offered throughout the week. Check the website or call for details.

Rudi Lechner's German-American Restaurant
2503 S. Gessner Rd., in Woodlake Square
(713) 782-1180
www.rudilechners.com

Feel like busting out your lederhosen? Celebrate Oktoberfest at Rudi Lechner's every Wednesday, when a German sampler buffet is offered from 6 to 9 p.m. The best part of this event? Live music from the band Alpenfest, which uses a 13-foot Swiss alphorn, a set of Austrian cowbells, a German xylophone, and yodeling to entertain the crowd. Audience participation, including the chicken dance, is an important part of the show. Live music is also offered Thurs through Sat starting at 6:30 p.m. The restaurant is open from 11:30 a.m. to 10 p.m. Mon through Sat. Menu items include stuffed cabbage rolls, escargot, quiche, a Hungarian goulash sampler, *kaesespatzle*, jaeger schnitzel, braised brisket, roasted pork loin, and beef tenderloin brochette. A variety of vegetarian options are also available.

Sam's Boat

5720 Richmond Ave.
(713) 781-2628
www.samsboat.com

The most recognizable thing about these local chain restaurant-bars is that the outside is shaped like, well, a giant boat. Once you go inside, however, you'll find a fun, inviting atmosphere, delicious Gulf Coast seafood, and live music most nights. Trust me: Whether you go for the music, the food, or the strong drinks, you'll enjoy yourself here. Additional locations are in Seabrook at 3101 NASA Rd. 1, Building B (281-326-7267), and in Montgomery at 15250 Hwy. 105 West, Suite 150 (936-588-1212).

Sambuca

909 Texas St.
(713) 224-5299
www.sambucarestaurant.com

With its location in the heart of downtown, Sambuca is a popular happy hour spot. But if you're craving a little live music, you're in luck, because this cool restaurant-lounge also has music seven nights a week. Music may range from pop, to classic rock, to jazz and Latin beats. The happy hour specials are great, too.

Spanish Flower Mexican Restaurant

4701 N. Main St.
(713) 869-1706

This twenty-four-hour Tex-Mex joint has been in the news a lot lately because Lady Gaga ate here when she was in town for her tour, but even without its celebrity clientele, this joint is worth a visit for its solid fare. Plus, it has live music every night featuring different musicians. Grab a seat on the huge patio and a margarita and enjoy. Popular menu items here include nachos, huevos rancheros, cheese enchiladas, and a $5.95 lunch special on weekdays from 10 a.m. to 10 p.m. Diners who order an entree during these hours will also receive a free bowl of soup.

The Tasting Room

1101 Uptown Park Blvd.
(713) 993-9800
www.tastingroomwines.com

Like a few tunes with your wine? You're in luck at the Tasting Room, which offers live music almost every day at both the Uptown Park location and the second site at 2409 W. Alabama St. (713-526-2242). Music ranges from acoustic rock to country to Latin grooves. Check the website for artists and times. Drink and food specials are also available.

Tied Fly Bar

2011 Ella Blvd., inside Rainbow Lodge
(713) 861-8666
www.rainbow-lodge.com

If you think something seems fishy about this rustic, 20-foot-long, U-shaped bar, you'd be right. It was built around a fish tank that spotlights hand-carved fake rainbow trout seemingly making their way downstream. But that's not the only thing unique about this popular bar. It also hosts fantastic live music from 6 to 9 p.m. every Friday night. It also offers a monthly wine dinner on the second Sunday of each month. The bar food menu includes slow-roasted Sicilian olives, duck gumbo with andouille sausage, green chili fries, and grilled chicken skewers.

Watson's House of Ales

14656 Grisby Rd.
(281) 920-2929
www.sherlockspubco.com

The Catch: On weekends a slight cover may be charged.

Part of the local Baker Street/Sherlock's chain, Watson's House of Ales offers live music Tues through Sat. Between that and its great happy hour, which is offered from 2 to 9 p.m. Tues through Sat and all day Sun and Mon, you can't really go wrong here. Happy hour specials include $2.00 domestic pints, $2.25 wells, $2.25 select premium domestic pints, $3.00 calls, $7.00 domestic pitchers, and $8.00 select premium domestic pitchers. Daily drink specials include $2.00 domestic drafts on Tues and $2.75 big beers and $3.75 imported big beers on Sat. Watson's is open from 11 a.m. to 2 a.m. daily.

FREE EXPRESSION:
OPEN MICS, POETRY READINGS & MORE

*"I think a poet is anybody
who wouldn't call himself a poet."*

—BOB DYLAN

Ever wanted to step up to the mic and try out that new joke, song, or poem you've been working on? After all, what do you have to lose (even if there's an "Is this thing on?" moment or two)? Thankfully, Houston is filled with places that offer weekly open mic nights, which are almost always free and open to the public. Here are some of the best places to get your talent on.

OPEN **MIC** NIGHTS

Avant Garden
411 Westheimer Rd.
(832) 519-1429
www.avantgardenhouston.com

This place is known for drawing artistic types, and even more come out on Tues, when the bar hosts Bards' Night Open Mic. "All good musicians" are welcome at this space; doors open at 7 p.m. and shows start at 9 p.m. Drink specials include $2 beers. Avant Garden also hosts a weekly wine tasting on Thurs. Call for details.

Blanco's
3406 W. Alabama St.
(713) 439-0072
www.houstonredneck.com/blancos.html

This beloved country bar puts its fate in your hands every Wednesday when it opens an open mic/jam night hosted by a different band each week. The band plays from 8 to 10 p.m., followed by open mic participants. No cover. Happy hour lasts from 11 a.m. to 9 p.m., and the kitchen closes at 10 p.m.

Bohemeos
708 Telephone Rd.
(713) 923-4277
www.bohemeos.com

This East End coffeehouse has slowly been attracting a nice following thanks to its tasty pastries, ice-cold beverages, and interesting clientele. The cafe hosts two open mic nights each week. The first, on Wed, takes place from 8 to 11 p.m. and is entirely Beatles themed (acoustic Beatles songs only; three-song limit). The second open mic is held on Sun from 8 to 11 p.m. and welcomes all styles of acoustic music and poetry. A ten-minute limit applies.

Crazy Frogs Saloon
17776 Tomball Parkway
(281) 894-1930
www.crazyfrogs.net

This sports bar offers a ton of weekly events including open mic night every Thurs. Other weekly events include free Texas hold 'em Mon through Thurs, karaoke Wed and Fri, free darts on Mon, pool tournaments on Tues, and live music on Sat. The bar is also always looking for amateur comedians to participate in comedy contests.

Fitzgerald's
2706 White Oak Dr.
(713) 862-7469
www.fitzlive.com

The open mic night at Fitzgerald's, called Rock Jam, gives you an opportunity to play the hallowed stage where so many local and touring acts have played before. Held every Wednesday night, Rock Jam gives up-and-coming artists a chance to try out their music in an acoustic setting (no drums or amps allowed). Admission is free; doors open at 8 p.m.

JP Hops House
2317 S. Hwy. 6
(281) 496-0623
www.jphopshouse.com

This pub boasts more than 150 beers, a "famous free popcorn buffet" (you have to go to try it), and a solid open mic night every Sun starting at 6 p.m. The bar is open from 3 p.m. to midnight on Sun and Mon, 3 p.m. to 1 a.m. Tues and Wed, and 3 p.m. to 2 a.m. Thurs through Sat.

Last Concert Cafe
1403 Nance St.
(713) 226-8563
www.lastconcert.com

Known for its concerts, this place also has a rockin' open mic night every Mon starting at 6 p.m. The kitchen is open on open mic night until 9 p.m.; drink specials are also available.

McGonigel's Mucky Duck
2425 Norfolk St.
(713) 528-5999
www.mcgonigels.com

It may be one of Houston's favorite laid-back concert venues, but every Monday it turns the table on its regulars by offering an open mic night at 7 p.m. (sign up is at 6:30 p.m.). Each performer is given fifteen minutes—or three songs—on stage. Original work and covers are welcome; comedians, poets, and other artists are also invited to take the stage.

Notsuoh
314 Main St.
(713) 409-4750
www.notsuoh.com

This funky little place (*Notsuoh* is *Houston* spelled backwards) hosts a variety of events throughout the week. The crowd is eclectic, smart, and sometimes intimidating, but also a wonderful mix of the type of people who make Houston special. One of the most popular nights here is open mic poetry night on Wednesday, when everyone from hipster students to sixty-something professors come out to state their minds. The place may confuse you, but as a Houston institution, it's also well worth the visit.

Sherlock's Baker Street Pub
1952 W. Gray St.
(713) 521-1881
www.sherlockspubco.com

Looking for a way to shake up your Sunday? Head to Sherlock's Baker Street Pub in River Oaks for the open mic comedy night, held every Sun starting around 9:30. Admission is free and drinks are on special (starting at $2) all night. Call ahead for details or to find out how to participate.

Taft Street Coffee
2115 Taft St.
(713) 522-3533
www.taftstreetcoffee.org

This great little cafe serves up "coffee with a conscience," as well as the largest offering of fair-trade beans in the city. Every Tuesday, the Taft Street space turns into an open mic poetry night for anyone with something to say. Pour out your heart and soul or simply watch with a hot cup of joe. Either way, you'll probably learn something. Other classes and special events are held throughout the week.

MEET & GREETS

Where to hear brilliant people speak (and maybe get an autograph or two).

Blue Willow Bookshop
14532 Memorial Dr.
(281) 497-8675
www.bluewillowbookshop.com

This local bookshop offers a nice mix of fiction and nonfiction and places an emphasis on recommending books that will appeal to both young and older customers. Service is warm and friendly, and gift wrap is free. Best-selling authors such as Sophie Jordan and Lauren Weisberger frequently offer free talks here; check the website for details.

Brazos Bookstore
2421 Bissonnet St.
(713) 523-0701
www.brazosbookstore.com

Opened in 1974, Brazos Bookstore has made it a mission to offer books that are both stimulating and relevant to the local community. The result is a diverse selection of books inside the store, a fiercely loyal clientele, and a steady flow of important authors who come by for book signings, lectures, and other events. Authors who have visited the store include Hana Samek

Norton, Olivia deBelle Byrd, and Pauline Frommer, to name a few. Author appearances are free.

Cactus Music
2110 Portsmouth St.
(713) 526-9272
www.cactusmusictx.com

Always a favorite spot among Houston's music lovers, Cactus Music also offers meet and greets, album signings, and Q & As with local and touring bands. Just check the calendar online for details and show up; events are always free. Even if your favorite band isn't coming through, you should still go by. This is a Houston institution.

Domy Books
1709 Westheimer Rd.
(713) 523-3669
www.domystore.com

Free movies are the name of the game here, where titles such as *Kung Fu Hustle, A Hard Day's Night,* and *Monty Python and the Holy Grail* are shown throughout the week. Oh, and did I mention this bookstore located off Westheimer Road also has a gallery? Progressive, hip, and interesting, this is the kind of place you want to check out for yourself. The emphasis here is on editioned books, periodicals, video, and products that focus on national and international contemporary art. You may not meet your favorite author here, but you'll find plenty of people who will want to discuss him or her with you.

HoustonPBS Elevate Lecture Series
4343 Elgin St.
(713) 748-8888
www.houstonpbs.org

HoustonPBS is known for its high-quality educational content, and every few months it furthers that mission by bringing in well-known personalities for its popular Elevate Lecture Series. Past participants have included Susie Gharib, Gwen Ifill, Rick Steves, and Bill Stubbs. Ticket prices vary. Check the website for upcoming speakers and prices.

Inprint Margarett Root Brown Reading Series
Readings take place at multiple
venues in Houston's downtown Theater District
(713) 521-2026
www.inprinthouston.org

Now in its thirtieth season, the Inprint Margarett Brown Reading Series regularly draws Pulitzer Prize winners, US poet laureates, Booker Prize recipients, and other literary heavyweights to Houston. Last year's lineup included authors such as Amy Tan, Carlos Fuentes, Salman Rushdie, and Peter Carey. All readings start at 7:30 p.m. General admission tickets are $5 for adults, free for seniors sixty-five and up and students.

Katy Budget Books
2450 Fry Rd.
(281) 578-7770
www.katybooks.com

Bargain hunters unite! This community bookstore offers a giant selection of new and used books and hosts occasional free events to encourage new customers to come into the store. Check this out as an alternative to the (also great) Half-Priced Books chain.

Murder By the Book
2342 Bissonnet St.
(713) 524-8597
www.murderbooks.com

As you could probably guess from its title, this specialty bookshop focuses on murder mysteries (the toll-free number here is (888-4-AGATHA). In addition to its large selection of mysteries, the store also hosts free lectures, book signings, and readings as well as a mystery author luncheon (tickets must be purchased for this event). Check the website for a listing of upcoming authors.

KARAOKE **NIGHTS**

Been a while since you belted out "Don't Stop Believing" to a group of tipsy co-workers? Never fear. Houston loves its karaoke, and it's got plenty of spots where you can perform. Whether you want to sing in a secluded private room with your best buds or channel your inner American Idol wannabe, you can do it in this city. Here's a sample of some of the best places to go.

Glitter Karaoke
2621 Milam St.
(713) 526-4900

Offering a much-needed outlet for karaoke in Midtown, Glitter slipped into the scene last year. It took a little while for them to get all of their ducks in a row, but now it's turned into a pretty solid little joint. Open on Tues and Thurs through Sun from 10 p.m. to 2 a.m., this is the perfect place to go for your night on the town, particularly after a few cheap drinks from nearby Christian's Tailgate.

Mezzanine Lounge
2200 Southwest Freeway
(713) 528-6399
www.mezzaninelounge.com

This bar-lounge is known for all kinds of weekly specials, but one of the most famous is its "extreme karaoke," which starts every Wed and Sat at 9:30 p.m. What is extreme karaoke, you ask? Good question. The trouble is, everyone gets so excited by the nightly drink specials, such as $2.50 domestic drafts and $3.50 Jack Daniels (depending on which night you go), that they never take the time to figure out what makes it so extreme. Either way, this place is solid fun and great place to go for a night out with friends.

Mix Karaoke
13151 Bissonnet St.
(281) 564-0500
www.mixkaraokelounge.com

The look of this cool, glossy karaoke lounge is impressive, but what's even more impressive is the song list, which includes more than 10,000 songs in

English, Chinese, and Vietnamese. It's open Wed through Sun from 8 p.m. to 2 a.m. for people age eighteen and up; admission is free for those twenty-one and older. Liquor and beer are served here, and a surprisingly decent bar menu is available. For a fee, you can also reserve the VIP room.

Spotlight Karaoke
5901 Westheimer Rd.
(713) 266-7768
www.spotlightkaraoke.com

The Catch: There's a $5 cover on weekends.

My personal favorite spot for karaoke, this place is filled with rooms perfect for all kinds of occasions. Having a night out with a few friends and want to show off those vocal chords? Sign up for a song on the main stage. Hosting a birthday party or bachelorette? Reserve a private room so you and your buddies can make fools of yourselves in the privacy of your own space. Either way, you're pretty much guaranteed to have a good time here. Spotlight Karaoke is open until 2 a.m. daily, with a two-drink minimum required to sing. An on-site sushi bar is also available.

The Tavern
1340 W. Gray St.
(713) 522-5152
www.thetavernongray.com

This great local bar has all kinds of special events, from poker night to steak night to live DJs. One of the most fun times to come here is on Tues, when karaoke starts at 9:30 p.m. Happy hour runs from 3 to 8 p.m. and includes $2 pints, $6 pitchers, and $3 frozen margaritas and Bellinis. Other amenities here include Ping-Pong tables, beer pong, foosball, and ample TVs.

LAUGH ATTACK:
COMEDY CLUBS

*"Comedy is the art of making people laugh
without making them puke."*

—STEVE MARTIN

They may not be fine art, but Houston's got a solid contingent of comedy clubs that can offer a nice change of pace on a Saturday night. (Just remember to avoid eye contact with the folks on stage, or you're likely to get called up into the action.) From colorful politicians to horrendous traffic to weird zoning laws, Houston's got plenty of fodder for those seeking a few belly laughs. Here's a sample of the best places to go.

Comedy Showcase
11460 Fuqua St.
(281) 481-1188
www.thecomedyshowcase.com

The club is a little grittier than the Improv, but the shows are just as solid, with a touring lineup that has included Miguel Washington, Craig Bush, Rick Gutierrez, and Sean Kent. Shows are held on Fri and Sat at 8 p.m. (seating begins at 7 p.m.) and 10:30 p.m. (seating begins at 9:45 p.m.). Food and drinks are available during shows. Call for ticket prices, which vary.

ComedySportz Houston
901 Town and Country Blvd.
(713) 868-1444
www.comedysportzhouston.com

What do you get when two teams of improv comics face off against one another in a heated battled of wits? ComedySportz, of course! This interactive comedy show is open to all ages and was designed to provide family-friendly, positive, good clean fun. Sound a little too clean? Don't worry—they also serve beer and wine in the 120-seat theater. Free parking is available. Tickets are $8 for matinees and $16 for evening shows; discounts are available for students, seniors, and military personnel. Children are welcome, although kids under six are not admitted to the 8 p.m. shows. There is also a late-night show at 10:30 p.m. on Sat for those age seventeen and up. Here's a tip: Join the ComedySportz Birthday Club and see a free match the month of your birthday.

Houston Comedy Union
Performs at various spots around town
http://houstoncomedyunion.wordpress.com

This scrappy yet impressive group prides itself on offering the most entertaining comedy-related open mics, movie nights, improv, and stand-up sets at select venues around town. Comprised of well-known Houston comics, it's worth the time to see a show. Not convinced? Performances are typically free and almost always are paired with fabulous drink specials. What's not to love?

Houston Comedy Film Festival

Alamo Drafthouse, 1000 West Oaks Mall
www.houstoncomedyfilmfestival.com

This annual three-day event held in December features dozens of hilarious short and feature-length independent films from across the globe. Tickets are less than $10 a night and get you nearly five hours worth of screenings. Just be sure to book in advance—last year's event included a sold-out show.

Improv Comedy Club

7620 Katy Freeway
(713) 333-8800
www.improv.com

The motto here is "where comedy begins," and with this national chain having helped launch the careers of—or at least played host to—celebrities such as Lily Tomlin, Adam Carolla, Aisha Tyler, Bill Engvall, Bill Maher, and Adam Sandler, that's probably true. During a visit to Houston's Improv, you can expect an evening of food, drinks, and laughs, as well as an awkward moment or two. Not into the late-night comedy scene? Check the online calendar for other events, such as an all-ages comedy and magic show that's offered occasionally. Tickets start around $15—not bad for a night out.

Laff Spot

8905 Louetta Rd., Spring
(281) 655-7777
www.laffspot.com

It's easy to confuse this joint with the Laff Stop, a legendary Houston comedy club that closed its doors in 2009, but this place is worthy of recognition in its own right thanks to its solid shows and fun atmosphere. With performances Thurs through Sun, the Laff Spot is becoming a go-to spot for a comedy fix. And with comedians such as Ron Shock, Patrick DeGuire, and Sam Demaris on the lineup, they're in good shape. Shows are 8 p.m. on Thurs; 8 and 10:30 p.m. on Fri; 7, 9, and 10:45 p.m. on Sat; and 8 p.m. on

Sun. Tickets are generally $15 with a two-item minimum purchase. Go to the website to print out a $5-off-per-ticket coupon.

Radio Music Theatre
2623 Colquitt St.
(713) 522-7722
www.radiomusictheatre.com

The name of the game at this little theater is sketch comedy produced by a three-person team portraying multiple members of the singing Fertle family. Shows blend comedy, satire, music, and drama, and watching one is like temporarily—and gladly—joining part of a traveling circus. Shows are held at 8:30 p.m. on Thurs, 8:30 p.m. on Fri, and at 8 and 10:30 p.m. on Sat. Reservations are recommended. Tickets are not particularly cheap—around $24—but this is one show that's worth the cash.

Third Coast Comedy
2317 W. 34th St.
(713) 263-9899
www.thirdcoastcomedy.com

Between its improv shows, original sketch comedy, and improv classes, you're bound to find something you like about this local comedy club. If you're looking for something fun to do on the weekend, try out one of the Friday or Saturday night improv shows, which incorporate audience suggestions and have a format similar to *Whose Line is it Anyway?* Tickets are $10 for adults and $5 for students and children. Check the website for more details.

FILM:
THE REEL DEAL

"If I can sell tickets to my movies like Red Sonja *or* Last Action Hero, *you know I can sell just about anything."*

—ARNOLD SCHWARZENEGGER

Is there anything better than a Friday night at the movies? The too-buttered popcorn. The worn-out seats. The overpriced tickets.

OK, so maybe the movie-going experience could be improved. If you're looking for something better than the norm, you have some alternatives here. Not only do Houston's independent movie houses bring in some of the coolest indie flicks, but they also offer amenities such as cocktails and kid-friendly options you may not find elsewhere. Here are some of the best places to go for a truly unique—and budget-friendly—night of film.

CHEAP & FREE SEATS

Aurora Picture Show
1524 Sul Ross St.
(713) 868-2101
www.aurorapictureshow.org

Calling itself a "nonprofit micro-cinema," the Aurora Picture Show offers creative, noncommercial film and video to a diverse mix of Houstonians and visitors. Founded in 1998, the nonprofit organization now hosts screenings and special events at a variety of interesting local spaces. Genres of screenings include history, children, art, Texas-based themes, and documentaries. A Houston original, an Aurora Picture Show screening is a must for all locals and visitors.

Discovery Green
1500 McKinney St.
(713) 400-7336
www.discoverygreen.com

A hub for all sorts of entertainment in Houston, Discovery Green is known for its free movie screenings, which have ranged from *Rushmore* to *The Wizard of Oz* to *Shrek*. In addition to offering wonderful screenings in a beautiful downtown setting, special movie events also frequently feature prizes, audience participation, giveaways, and more. Check the online calendar for a list of upcoming options.

River Oaks Theatre
2009 W. Gray St.
(713) 866-8881
www.landmarktheatres.com

Perhaps the most beloved theater in Houston, River Oaks regularly brings in the best independent, foreign, and just plain fun films to Houston. It also hosts frequent special events, such as live performances of *The Rocky Horror Picture Show*. Don't miss the chance to see a show at this local institution, which also happens to have a full bar. Ticket prices are average, but the experience is priceless.

The Showboat Drive-In
22422 FM 2920, Hockley
(281) 351-5224
www.theshowboatdrivein.com

Seeking a throwback to the good old days? Then the Showboat Drive-In is the place for you. For just $5 you get a double feature of some of the newest releases. Just pay (cash only), park, turn your radio to the correct station, and enjoy. Open Fri through Sun. Gates open at 7 p.m.; the first show starts at dusk. Kids ages three through twelve are $4; babies are free. Trust me, on a nice night with the windows down, you can't beat an evening here. Go for a date or take the whole family—it'll be cheaper than pretty much anything else you can find.

DINNER & A **MOVIE:** ON **THE** CHEAP

Alamo Drafthouse
2600 Hwy. 6 South
(281) 920-9211
www.drafthouse.com

This Texas-based chain features new releases and cult classics in a restaurant-like atmosphere. You go in, pick a seat, and take a look at the menu placed on the table in front of you. Feel like ordering some grub or a stiff drink? Write your order on the supplied paper and leave it for your server. A few minutes later, voila! Food, drinks, and flicks. Simple as that. The theater also frequently hosts special events such as TV show–viewing parties and baby days, where parents can bring little ones without anyone making a fuss, plus admission is free for children under six. An additional Houston-area location is in Katy at 531 S. Mason Rd. (281-398-5454).

Movie Tavern
15719 I-45 North
(281) 248-8396
www.movietavern.com

The Movie Tavern offers a full-service restaurant, bar, and lounge concept that serves up food and drinks as you watch the latest movie releases. Locations also offer special events such as all-you-can-eat flapjacks and family movies at 9 a.m. on Sat, occasional retro flicks such as *Ghostbusters* and *Goonies,* and 3-D films when available. Additional locations are at 18359 Tomball Parkway (832-678-2171) and 9630 FM 1960 Bypass West, Humble (281-446-6319).

Studio Movie Grill
805 Town and Country Lane at CityCentre
(713) 461-4449
www.studiomoviegrill.com

Want a real bite to eat while you watch your movie? Then head to Studio Movie Grill, where menu options include items such as gourmet pizza, quesadillas, and salads, as well as a full bar. From the latest movies to family-friendly and special-needs screenings, you're sure to find something here that will entertain your whole brood. Tickets are comparable to other theaters featuring new releases, and the service here is solid. A second location is at 8580 Hwy. 6 North at West Road (832-593-6684).

SECTION 2:

Living in Houston

FOOD:
ALL YOU CAN EAT

"Never eat more than you can lift."

— MISS PIGGY

Is there anything more wonderful than free food? Yes—delicious free food. And in this town there are tons of places to find it, from bars to farmers' markets to superstores. And this is more than just free bar popcorn, too. We're talking meal material. Here are some of the best places to get your nosh on in town.

SAMPLING **SENSATIONS**

Looking for just a nibble, or seven? Check out these supermarkets and specialty stores, which are known for their generous samples.

Central Market
3815 Westheimer Rd.
(713) 386-1700
www.centralmarket.com

This expansive specialty grocery store is known for its variety of culinary treasures, and also for its generosity in sharing them with the general public. On any given day (particularly on weekends) you're likely to grab a taste of offerings such as fresh-squeezed juice, homemade salsa, just-grilled fish, tender tortillas, chunky cookies, exotic produce, and locally made gelato, to name a few. If that doesn't satisfy your appetite, grab a seat in the on-site cafe or grab lunch from the wide to-go coolers. For even better luck, time your visit with a special event, such as the Hatch Chile Festival or the Taste of Argentina, when there's practically a sample per square foot.

Costco
1150 Bunker Hill Rd.
(713) 576-2050
www.costco.com

Granted, you already know about Costco. You love it for its bulk goods, you love it for the variety of items it sells, and you love it for its samples. But because this place is such a Mecca for free-food seekers, its worth saying again that if you want to leave a store full after a shopping experience, this is the place to do it. Costco offers copious samples throughout its famed warehouses—particularly on Saturday—that may range from chicken wings to cookies to bread. Hungry for more? You can score a hot dog and a Coke for $1.50. Just bring cash, your Amex credit card, or a Costco Cash card—those are the only types of payment accepted. Additional locations are at 3836 Richmond Ave. (832-325-5850) and 12405 N. Gessner Rd. (832-912-2353).

H-E-B Buffalo Market
5225 Buffalo Speedway
(713) 218-1800
www.heb.com

This regional grocery store chain is a local favorite for its fresh goods and affordable prices, but when the Buffalo Speedway location opened in 2008, it upped the game in a major way. Designed as an upscale version of its usual stores, H-E-B Buffalo Market has gourmet to-go items, hundreds of types of cheese, 2,000 types of wine, and cooking and sushi stations. On top of that, it has tons of sample stations, meaning you've got a great chance of walking out full when you go there. If you want to take something home, don't miss the delicious (and affordable) precooked frozen meals.

Hubbell & Hudson
24 Waterway Ave., Suite 125, The Woodlands
(281) 203-5600
www.hubbellandhudson.com

This gourmet market is a gold mine for both imported and house-made goodies. A tour through the store includes a bakery with artisan breads and pastries, a European-style deli, a produce area filled with local, organically grown fruits and veggies, a coffee kiosk, a huge seafood department, and rare cheeses and charcuterie, all of which regularly offer samples. Want to know what's even better? The store happily embraces a "sip and shop" philosophy, where customers are encouraged to grab a glass of wine or beer to drink as they make their way around the store. Now you really can have your treats and drink them, too.

Spec's
2410 Smith St.
(713) 526-8787
www.specsonline.com

It may be Houston's favorite liquor store, but the downtown headquarters of this local chain is also filled with hard-to-find goodies such as chocolate, caviar, cheese, and meat that are frequently out for sample. If you like what you taste, stick around for lunch of one of the on-site daily lunch specials. And don't miss Friday afternoons, when the store transforms into an amazing food-and-booze fest with samples around every turn. Decide to buy something? Pay with cash (or debit card) and you'll save even more.

Whole Foods
6401 Woodway Dr.
(713) 789-4477
www.wholefoodsmarket.com

This Texas-based chain is stocked with delicious finds. Known for its healthy and organic fare, you can expect to find ample samples here at any time of day. The bakery, cheese, and butcher areas are particularly good places to score a tasty bite, but other areas offer them as well. Check the website for special events, tastings, classes, listing information for their four other Houston-area locations, and more.

FREE FOOD

You can't beat a good meal, and when you can get one without shelling out any dough at all, that's even better. Thankfully, Houston has a lot of such places. Here are some of the best places to score a free bite.

Chuy's Comida Deluxe
2706 Westheimer Rd.
(713) 524-1700
www.chuys.com

This popular Tex-Mex joint has always had a fun, quirky atmosphere, delicious drinks, and mouthwatering fare. And during happy hour from 4 to 7 p.m., the restaurant also offers a self-serve build-your-own nacho bar with mounds of crispy chips and toppings such as queso, salsa, beans, meat, and more. Wash it down with $3.50 margaritas, $2.50 domestic beers, and $6.95 house Texas martinis. For more information on their four other Houston-area locations, check out Chuy's website.

Howl at the Moon
612 Hadley St.
(713) 658-9700
www.howlatthemoon.com

The Catch: You must pay a $7 cover to get through the door.

TGIF! The end of the work week gets even sweeter at Howl at the Moon, a dueling piano bar that offers a complimentary appetizer buffet every Fri from 5 to 8 p.m. Drinks are also half off during this time. The dueling piano show starts at 6 p.m.

Los Cucos Mexican Cafe
17886 Northwest Freeway
(713) 849-0061
www.loscucos.com

Enjoy a free taco bar and appetizer specials when you visit this Houston-area Tex-Mex chain during happy hour from 3 to 6 p.m. The drink specials are almost as good as the food deals. On Mon and Tues, get $1.59 margaritas all day; on Wed, Thurs, and Fri they are $3.50 during happy hour. Draft beers are 99 cents during happy hour. Check out the website for listing information on their many locations.

Osaka Japanese Restaurant
515 Westheimer Rd.
(713) 533-9098

If you love free food, Osaka Japanese Restaurant is the place to go. Not only will $10 get you a great sampling of delectable sushi, but when you dine here, you'll almost always get a free appetizer such as dumplings and shrimp tempura and free ice cream in flavors such as green tea, plum, and ginger for dessert. All that plus an extremely friendly staff make this a place to try over and over again.

t'afia
3701 Travis St.
(713) 524-6922
www.tafia.com

This beloved Houston institution gets even better at happy hour Tues through Thurs, when items from its wide happy hour menu are free with purchase of an alcoholic beverage. Complimentary bites include savory options such as organic edamame, chickpea "fries," cocktail burgers, and sashimi; sweet nibbles include chocolate truffles, mascarpone dates, and pumpkin cheese-cake. Items may change; call ahead for specifics.

Taps House of Beer
5120 Washington Ave.
(281) 701-4248
www.tapshouseofbeer.com

Nestled within Houston's uber-trendy Washington Avenue district, Taps House of Beer is a refreshingly low-key addition to the neighborhood. With its wide selection of beers, cool vibe (shuffleboard and dominos are among its amenities), and beer-smart bartenders, you're likely to enjoy this place. Every Tuesday, taps serves free hot dogs and $2 Texas beers all night.

The Tasting Room—River Oaks
2409 W. Alabama St.
(713) 526-2242
www.tastingroomwines.com

The Catch: You must register at www.theblackdoor.com to qualify.

This cool wine room offers more than 150 wines ranging in price from $15 to more than $1,000 a bottle. But if you're looking for a deal, head over on Sun and Mon, when the purchase of a bottle of wine gets you a free gourmet pizza to enjoy at the bar. The deal is available on Sun from 3 to 9 p.m. and Mon from 3 to 11 p.m.

West Alabama Ice House
1919 W. Alabama St.
(713) 528-6874
www.westalabamaicehouse.com

This dog- and kid-friendly joint is one of Houston's favorite spots to grab a cold brew. Whether you have a seat at an outside picnic table, play a quick game of pool, shoot some hoops, or toss some horseshoes, this is the place to come on a nice spring or fall day. And should you get hungry, you're in luck, because on Friday nights, the bar also serves up free hot dogs and live local music. All major credit cards are accepted.

Wild West Houston
6101 Richmond Ave.
(713) 266-2282
www.wildwesthouston.com

This huge bar may be known for its wide dance floor and cheap longnecks, but it also has a darn good Sunday happy hour that includes a free fajita dinner. Just show up for free dance lessons from 4:30 to 6 p.m. and enjoy a solid spread of fajitas and all the trimmings afterward. Want something to wash down the Tex-Mex deliciousness? Bottled beer, wine, and call drinks are just $2.50.

CHEAP **EATS**

Sure, free food may be great, but cheap food isn't bad, either. And if you know the right time to go, you can find some incredible deals at some of Houston's best eateries. Here are some of my favorites.

Benjy's
2424 Dunstan Rd.
(713) 522-7602
www.benjys.com

Known for its sexy atmosphere, attractive clientele, and hip food, this isn't the first place you'd expect to have great happy hour specials. But it does. Every night from 4 to 7 p.m., Benjy's offers a $5 happy hour menu featuring everything from calamari, to tomato and spinach crepes, to homemade chicken sausage pizza, to pork pot stickers. Discounted drinks, such as $5 wines and cocktails, are also available. A second location is at 5922 Washington Ave. (713-868-1131).

Branch Water Tavern
510 Shepherd Dr.
(713) 863-7777
www.branchwatertavern.com

One of the newer restaurants to the scene, Branch Water Tavern proudly serves up "artisanal American food and drink." During happy hour, which is weekdays from 4 to 7 p.m., that means tasty interesting food at a discounted price. A sample of the offerings includes $3 duck-fat popcorn, $1 Reuben sliders, $4 crispy stuffed olives, $1 oysters on the half shell, and $5 duck-liver mousse. Drink specials are equally as good, with a $3 daily whiskey drink of choice, $2 beers, and $5 you call its.

Cadillac Bar
1802 Shepherd Dr.
(713) 862-2020
www.cadillacbar.com

The Catch: Food specials are available at the bar only.

It may be known for its margaritas, but the happy hour grub at this centrally located bar is also worth the trip. Offerings include $3 chicken quesadillas and $4 *taquitos,* nachos, Mexican pizza, and stuffed jalapeños between 2 and 7 p.m. on weekdays. Drink specials include $2.00 domestic beer, $2.00 well drinks, $2.75 imports, half-priced wine, $3.50 margaritas, and $4.00 martinis.

Catalan Food & Wine
5555 Washington Ave.
(713) 426-4260
www.catalanfoodandwine.com

When one of the best restaurants in Houston begins offering a $5 "street food" happy hour menu from 4 to 7 p.m. Tues through Fri and from 5 to 7 p.m. on weekends, you go. Selections from the special menu have included roasted Berkshire pork belly with Steen's pure cane syrup, Gulf shrimp beignets over a spicy Tabasco mash remoulade, seared tuna with cucumber and red chile sake vinaigrette, and roasted flat bread with local tomatoes, goat cheese, and basil. They will change weekly, so call ahead if you're interested in something in particular. Catalan also offers drink specials such as $5.00 wells, $2.50 St. Arnold beers, and $1.75 Lone Star longnecks.

Courses Restaurant
Art Institute of Houston
1900 Yorktown St.
(713) 353-3644
www.artinstitutes.edu

Enjoy an upscale lunch of gumbo, roasted chicken, grilled salmon, flatiron steak, or penne pasta at Courses Restaurant, where aspiring student chefs

Hey Cupcake!

Nothing is more precious—and more affordable—than a cupcake. And thanks to the cupcake craze that continues to sweep the nation, there are nearly a dozen places to get your sweet fix in town. Take your pick of flavors, from classics such as yellow cake with chocolate frosting to bizarre new additions such as maple bacon. Feeling ready to satisfy that sweet tooth? Look no further.

Dessert Gallery

3600 Kirby Dr.

(713) 522-9999

www.dessertgallery.com

It's popular for its giant slices of cake, chocolate-dipped cookies, and boxed lunches, but Dessert Gallery also serves up one heck of a cupcake. Wrapped in pretty little papers that'll keep your fingers from getting messy, these classy little morsels are a decadent do any time you're in the neighborhood. Flavors change regularly—call stores for daily offerings. A second location is at 1616 Post Oak Blvd. (713-622-0008).

Frosted Betty Bake Shop

5806 Fourth St., Katy

(832) 437-5247

www.frostedbetty.com

Baked from scratch daily using local organic ingredients, Frosted Betty aims to incorporate community into every cupcake. Expect flavors such as carrot cake, coconut almond, salted caramel, Neopolitan, maple bacon, and white Russian. The store also owns a mobile bake shop—current locations can be found on Twitter at twitter.com/luv FrostedBetty.

Ooh La La Sweets

23920 Westheimer Parkway, Katy

(281) 391-2253

www.oohlalasweets.com

It's about a thirty-minute haul to Katy, but it's worth the trip for these adorable cupcakes. Hit up the drive-through (that's right, there's a cupcake drive through!) or design your own creation at the cupcake bar. Flavors include birthday cake, brown sugar cinnamon, ultimate chocolate, s'mores, and Boston crème pie. Whole cakes, pastries, cookies, and coffee are also available.

Sprinkles Cupcakes
1404 Westheimer Rd.
(713) 871-9929
www.sprinkles.com
Perhaps the buzziest of the local cupcake shops is Sprinkles Cupcakes, an L.A.-based chain that arrived in Houston last year. First off, they're adorable, with their neat wrappers and perfectly piped icing caps. More than that, they're delicious, melting in your mouth upon first bite. The fun flavors, which include chocolate marshmallow, key lime, pumpkin, and vegan red velvet, don't hurt either. The $3.25 price tag isn't the cheapest around, but it's well worth it.

Sugarbaby's Cupcake Boutique
3310 S. Shepherd Dr.
(713) 527-8427
www.ilovesugarbabys.com
With its precious pink-and-black decor and its wide range of treats, Sugarbaby's impresses. One of the first shops to jump on the cupcake trend in Houston, Sugarbaby's continues to do it right with solid service and sweets. Cupcake offerings include German chocolate, lemon raspberry, orange crème, and St. Arnold's root beer float. The store also serves other desserts including cheesecake, tarts, and cakes, as well as gourmet coffee, candy, and gifts.

What's Up Cupcake
Weekends at W. 14th Street and North Shepherd Drive
www.whatsupcupcake-houston.com
Taking a cue from Austin's incredible food truck scene, What's Up Cupcake rolls out the sweet treats from a trailer window every weekend. Flavors include organic chocolate truffle, strawberry berry berry good, butter cake with chocolate frosting, and Coca-Cola fudge. Plans for a What's Up Cupcake storefront are also in the works.

prepare deeply discounted meals under the direction of chef instructors. Most meals are half the price of what you would find at fine restaurants and just as delicious. The restaurant is open from 11 a.m. to 1 p.m. Mon through Thurs. Make reservations in advance.

Empire Cafe
1732 Westheimer Rd.
(713) 528-5282
www.empirecafe.com

This laid-back cafe serves delicious coffee drinks (with free cookies!) and a wide menu seven days a week to crowds that love its diverse yet comfortable offerings. But if you're craving something sweet, you've got to go on Monday, when slices of their gigantic, tender, sugar-filled creations are half off. Try flavors such as Toll House, lemon poppy seed, carrot, chocolate Italian cream, chocolate blackout, Berry White, and more. Trust me—for cake, you can't beat it.

Ikea Houston
7810 Katy Freeway
(713) 688-7867
www.ikea.com

You may know about the Swedish meatballs, but did you know that Ikea's restaurant also offers other specials such as a weekly Wednesday rib night (half rack with French fries and corn bread for $7.99) from 6 p.m. to closing time; a daily 99 cent breakfast deal from 9:30 to 11 a.m. that includes scrambled eggs, bacon, and Swedish potatoes; a coffee and cinnamon bun for $1.49; entrees such as chicken marsala for $4.99; and penne pasta with marinara or Alfredo sauce for $1.99? It does, and after a long morning or afternoon of shopping, it's sure to hit the spot.

Indika
516 Westheimer Rd.
(713) 524-2170
www.indikausa.com

This Indian restaurant prides itself on using local ingredients, and it shows in the quality of food the staff turns out. During happy hour, which runs from 5 to 7:30 p.m. on weekdays, the restaurant offers half off the bar food menu, which includes options such as chicken wings, a lentil and spinach burger, fish head cutlets, bread *pakora,* masala toast, and chicken tikka masala. Drinks are also half price.

Jasper's
9595 Six Pines Dr., Suite 900
The Woodlands
(281) 298-6600
www.kentrathbun.com

The Catch: The $5 deals are only offered in the bar and bar patio areas.

Created by renowned chef Kent Rathbun, Jasper's serves up amazing "gourmet backyard cuisine." And Sun through Thurs, you can get much of that cuisine for a mere $5. Offered all day on Sun and weekdays from 11 a.m. to 7 p.m. and from 9 p.m. to closing time, the $5 specials include items such as crostini, pulled-pork flautas, and more. Drink specials include $5 cocktails and $2 off beer and wine. The restaurant also offers a $35 four-course menu Sun through Thurs.

La Griglia
2002 West Gray St.
(713) 526-4700
www.lagrigliarestaurant.com

I'm not going to lie—this place is a *scene,* and definitely not the kind of place you'd expect to find a bargain. With the $20 salads on the menu, the B-list celebrities wandering the main room, and the BMWs, Mercedes, and Lexuses parked out front, it's a place that seems to radiate wealth. Except when it comes to the happy hour menu. On weekdays between 3 and 6 p.m., it turns into a frugal person's dream, with a full battery of half-price appetizers and dishes such as gnocchi alla Bolognese, meatball pizza, Romano-crusted veal, and lacquered salmon. Drink specials include $6 specialty martinis, $6 signature drinks, $5 wines, and $4 beers. A similar late-night menu is also available on select days.

Lucky Strike Lanes
1201 San Jacinto St.
(713) 343-3300
www.bowlluckystrike.com

On weekdays from 3 to 7 p.m. and Sun through Thurs from 10 p.m. to closing time, Lucky Strike Lanes rolls out happy hour specials that include half-
price appetizers (think sliders, Asian chicken skewers, and tuna lollipops)
as well as $5 cosmos and lemontinis, $4 house wine, and $3 Bud Light draft.
Another great deal is the Sunday brunch, which is held from 11 a.m. to 4
p.m. A mere $15 gets you bottomless mimosas and Bloody Marys, an entree,
and a free game of bowling and shoes.

Max's Wine Dive
4720 Washington Ave.
(713) 880-8737
www.maxswinedive.com

One of the coolest upscale gourmet restaurants in Houston gets a little more
affordable during its happy hour Mon through Thurs between 4 and 7 p.m.
and on Fri from 1 to 7 p.m. Specials include pulled-pork sliders for $7, truffle
chips for $6, and southern-fried turkey bites for $7. Typically drink specials,
such as $5 champagne, are also offered. There's also a reverse happy hour
Tues through Fri from midnight to 2 a.m.

McCormick and Schmick's
1151 Uptown Park Blvd.
(713) 840-7900
www.mccormickandschmicks.com

The Catch: There is a $3.50 minimum beverage purchase per person.

Sure, it's a chain, but it's also one of the best places for solid happy hour
grub in the city. During happy hour on weeknights between 4 and 7 p.m.
look for deals such as $1.95 salmon crostini, $2.95 half-pound cheeseburgers, and $3.95 pizza, mussels, fish tacos, and calamari. The drinks specials
are just as good, with $3.95 ZiegenBock draft, $4.95 sangria, and $5.95
house wine. Specials and food offerings vary by location; check the website
for details. Additional locations are at 1201 Fannin St. (713-658-8100) and
791 Town & Country Blvd. (713-465-3685).

Movie Tavern
15719 I-45 North
(281) 248-8396
www.movietavern.com

Concession stand prices at the movies may be quite a bit higher these days than in years past, but at least there's one place where you can still find a good deal: Movie Tavern. Every Saturday and Sunday morning at 9 a.m., Movie Tavern locations offer Flapjacks and a Flick, where you get a movie ticket, drinks, and all-you-can-eat pancakes for just $10.50 for adults and $9.00 for kids. Additional locations are in Houston at 18359 Tomball Parkway (832-678-2171) and in Humble at 9630 FM 1960 Bypass West (281-446-6319).

Pappasito's Cantina
Multiple Houston locations
www.pappasitos.com

This local chain always serves up amazing Tex-Mex fare, but on Wednesday the restaurants kick it into overdrive for half-price fajita night. If you go, expect to wait at least half an hour. It's worth it, though. Mariachis entertain the crowd, balloons attached to chairs entertain the little ones, and the food, once it arrives, is mouthwatering. If you really want to get a good deal, head up to the bar, order a round of drinks, and place a to-go order for the fajitas. You still get the same great price—beef or chicken fajitas for two for $16.25 (rice, beans, guacamole, tortillas and chips, and salsa included) without all the fuss. Plus, that way you don't have to leave as much of a tip. *Perfecto!*

Perry's Steakhouse and Grille
487 Bay Area Blvd.
(281) 286-8800
www.perrysrestaurants.com

During Perry's Social Hour at Bar 79 (aka happy hour) from 4 p.m. to 6:30 p.m., you can enjoy delicious half-price appetizers such as escargot, fried asparagus with colossal lump crabmeat, and smoked-pork quesadillas, as well as discounted wine and martinis. With so many locations in the Houston area (check out their website for listing information), you're bound to find one near you. With prices like this, it's a can't miss.

Ra Sushi

3908 Westheimer Rd.
(713) 621-5800
www.rasushi.com

This popular sushi restaurant offers a fantastic happy hour on weekdays from 3 to 7 p.m. that includes half-price appetizers (think tempura, chicken yakitori, and scallops) and discounts on certain rolls, as well as great drink specials. Sure, the Westheimer location borders on trendy to the point of obnoxious, but the food—and happy hour specials—are well worth the visit. A second location is at 12860 Queensbury Lane (713-331-2792).

Sacred Heart Society

816 E. Whitney St.
(713) 692-0198

If you like Italian food the way it was meant to be made, you can't miss the Thursday spaghetti and meatball lunch at the Sacred Heart Society. From 11 a.m. to 1 p.m., the society dishes out some of the best Italian fare you've ever had. The meal includes everything: spaghetti, salad, garlic bread, Italian sausage, and pigs' feet (yes, pigs' feet). The atmosphere is like something out of *The Sopranos,* and as an added bonus, there are door prizes. Beer and wine are also available. The full meal will cost you less than $10; a portion of the proceeds goes to charity.

Smith & Wollensky

4007 Westheimer Rd.
(713) 621-7555
www.smithandwollensky.com

This upscale steak house offers an impressive happy hour from 4 to 7 p.m. weekdays in the bar. Specials include $6 spicy fries with truffle mayo, $7 fried oysters with basil remoulade, $6 tomato and mozzarella flat bread, and $9 Wollensky's Butcher Burger with smoked apple-wood bacon, Vermont white cheddar cheese, and steak sauce mayo. Drink specials include $4 Shiner and Miller Lite bottles, $4 house wines, $7 Absolut martinis, and $7 prickly pear margaritas.

FARMERS' MARKETS

In a foodie city such as Houston, we're lucky to have a variety of great farmers' markets. Here are the best:

Houston Farmers' Market
Onion Creek Coffee House
3106 White Oak Blvd.
www.localharvest.org

Every Sat from 8 a.m. to noon, Onion Creek Coffee House hosts a great little farmers' market featuring food from local farmers that has been raised sustainably or organically.

Midtown Farmers' Market
t'afia
3701 Travis St.
www.tafia.com

Calling itself a "foodie paradise and morning party" all in one, this weekly farmers' market is held outside of renowned chef Monica Pope's restaurant, t'afia, every Sat from 8 a.m. to noon. Expect hot breakfast, mimosas, fresh-baked breads, cheeses, and on-site knife sharpening.

Rice University Farmers' Market
2100 University Blvd.
http://farmersmarket.rice.edu

Conveniently located on the Rice University campus, this farmers' market is dedicated to being an outlet for local farmers and a place for the public to find fabulous organic and locally grown food. Vendors offer a range of products including produce, fish, free-range eggs, gluten-free baked goods, coffee, soaps, cheese, and more. The market is held every Tues from 3:30 to 7 p.m.

Urban Harvest Farmers' Market at Discovery Green
1500 McKinney St.
(713) 880-5540
www.urbanharvest.org

Looking for something to do on a Sunday afternoon? Head to this farmers' market, conveniently located at Discovery Green, Houston's favorite urban park, from noon to 4 p.m. Expect everything from fresh tomatoes to handmade cheese to fresh-baked cookies. The market is held rain or shine.

Urban Harvest Farmers' Market at Eastside
3000 Richmond
(713) 880-5540
www.urbanharvest.org

This farmers' market offers a wide variety of locally produced veggies, fruits, seafood, baked goods, meats, and more from dozens of vendors in the Houston area. It is also a favorite spot among Houston chefs, who tend to congregate there. It is held every Sat from 8 a.m. to noon, rain or shine.

WHERE'S **THE** BEEF?

There are three things Texans love: beef, brews, and bars. In Houston there is nothing better than spending a nice evening on a patio, enjoying a cold beer and a world-class steak for a fraction of what you'd pay at one of the fancy steak places in town. When it comes to steak nights, you've got your choice of options. Here are some of the most popular.

Brian O'Neill's Irish Pub
5555 Morningside Dr.
(713) 522-2603
www.brianoneills.com

If you like steak, you'll want to head to Brian O'Neill's on Saturday for the "bigger and better" steak night, starting at 5 p.m. For $14.95 you'll get a fourteen-ounce rib eye with vegetable medley and loaded baked potato. Drink specials, which are offered Tues through Sat from 3 to 9 p.m. and Sun through Mon from 11 a.m. to 2 a.m., include $1.75 wells, $2.00 house wine, $2.00 domestic drafts, $2.25 Shiner draft, $6.00 domestic pitchers, $7.00 Shiner pitchers, and $7.00 Amstel Light pitchers. Other food specials are also offered throughout the week.

Brixx Houston
5110 Washington Ave.
(713) 864-8811
www.brixxhouston.com

It may be on the super trendy Washington Avenue, but Brixx's steak night is worth the trouble. Every Tues, the bar offers steak with a baked potato from 7 to 10 p.m. for $15. Other weekly specials include all-you-can-eat crawfish (seasonal) on Sat and drink specials throughout the week.

Kelvin Arms
2424 Dunstan Rd.
(713) 528-5002
www.kelvinarms.com

Craving meat? Drop by Kelvin Arms, where steak night rules every Tues and Thurs from 7 to 10 p.m. A rib eye and blue cheese potato salad will set you back just $12. Happy hour runs from 3 to 7 p.m. Tues through Sat, all day on Sun, and from 3 to 10 p.m. on Mon, and it includes $3 wells, $2 Miller and Bud Light drafts, and $1 off all other draft beer.

Little Woodrow's
5611 Morningside Dr.
(713) 521-2337
www.littlewoodrows.com

An ice house known for serving up "mucho cerveza, baby," Little Woodrow's also offers steak on its outdoor decks on certain nights of the week. On Wed at the Bellaire Boulevard location, get a sixteen-ounce rib eye, baked potato, and beer or wine for under $20. The bar also offers $2 "big ass" twenty-three-ounce draft beers on Wed. Coincidence? I think not. Steak night comes to the Midtown location (2306 Brazos St., 713-522-1041) on Thurs. Live turtle racing is also available on Thurs nights. Trust me, you don't want to miss it. A third location is at 4235 Bellaire Blvd. (713-661-5282).

Sing for Your Supper: Sunday Dinners

Sure, you know all about Sunday brunches. Practically every place in town has some approximation of one. Rather than offering eggs, bacon, and French toast, several places in town are encouraging you to save yourself for a proper Sunday dinner. From fried chicken to macaroni and cheese, these comfort dishes will get you all fueled up for the work week. Here are five of the best Sunday dinners to try.

Benjy's

2424 Dunstan Rd.

(713) 522-7602

www.benjys.com

This hip restaurant-lounge also serves a killer "Sunday supper" it calls "Benjy's take on comfort food." The menu features classics such as fried chicken with farmers' market salad and mom's chocolate cake. Three courses are $19 a person. Dinner is served at both locations from 5 to 9 p.m. every Sun. A second location is at 5922 Washington Ave. (713-868-1131).

BRC Gastro Pub

519 Shepherd Dr.

(713) 861-2233

www.brcgastropub.com

This gastro pub has been making waves since it opened last year thanks to its innovative American cuisine and fabulous beer and wine lists. Now, it's added a Sunday dinner option that's worth blowing off church for. It's a fried-chicken dinner for four, served with coleslaw and baked beans. It'll run you $60 (total), but it's worth every dollar. Plus, if you break it down, that's $15 a person for dinner at a moderate/upscale joint. Not bad.

Frank's Chop House

3736 Westheimer Rd.

(713) 572-8600

www.frankschophouse.com

You can always count on Frank's for fantastic Italian food, but now you can also depend on this Westheimer Road restaurant for a great Sunday dinner. Offered from 5 to 9 p.m. every Sun, the dinner includes half-price wine and a buttermilk fried-chicken special. Yum.

Rainbow Lodge

2011 Ella Blvd.

(713) 861-8666

www.rainbow-lodge.com

Rainbow Lodge has always had a faithful brunch following, but now the restaurant is hoping to convert some of those diners to its Sunday suppers, which include a "comfort food special" (in addition to the regular menu) and half-price wine by the glass after 5 p.m.

RDG + Bar Annie

1800 Post Oak Blvd.

(713) 840-1111

www.rdgbarannie.com

The recently remodeled RDG is one of the most beloved restaurants in Houston, and you can bet that the Sunday dinner here is well worth writing home to Mom about. The menu, which incorporates a "relaxation mode" vibe, includes community dishes such as black bean dip, Asian nachos, and chicken liver mousse with fig toast; traditions such as crispy rolled chicken tacos and slow-cooked beef rib enchiladas; and "Sunday plates" such as rainbow trout with crab meat and pine nut butter, roasted chicken, and steak and fries. Specialities, such as martinis and smoked oysters and cold beer and Gulf shrimp, are also offered. Call for hours and reservations.

Lucky's Pub
801 Saint Emanuel St.
(713) 522-2010
www.luckyspub.com

This place may have great drinks, but they also know how to cook up a mean steak. Every Tues is steak and pint night, where you can get a twelve-ounce rib eye for $12.95, a twelve-ounce rib eye and domestic pint for $14.95, or a twelve-ounce rib eye and a premium cocktail for $17.00.

Onion Creek Coffee House
3106 White Oak Dr.
(713) 880-0706
www.onioncreekcafe.com

This beloved Heights establishment offers one of the best steak nights in town every Wed from 6 to 10 p.m., when $15 will get you a rib eye, baked potato, and all the fixin's. Can't make it on Wednesday? Try a different special, such as the Monday Cajun shrimp boil or the waffles, made fresh every morning from 8 a.m. to noon.

PJ's Sports Bar
614 W. Gray St.
(713) 520-1748
www.pjssportsbar.com

This little sports bar is known for its big steak night held every Thurs, when $27 will get you two steaks, two potatoes, two salads, and a pitcher of beer. An extra pitcher will cost you $5. Other weekly specials include $6 pitchers on Sun and Mon until 11 p.m. and happy hour until 7 p.m. on Fri and Sat.

Red Lion Pub
2316 S. Shepherd Dr.
(713) 782-3030
www.redlionhouston.com

You'd expect a British pub to do steak night right, and this one does. Every Thurs, $20 will get you a filet mignon dinner with all the fixin's. Other weekly specials include $7 cheeseburgers on Mon, $18 curry and a pint on Wed, and $12 fish plates on Fri.

Sixth Street Bar and Grill
2701 White Oak Dr.
(713) 880-5999
www.6thstreetintheheights.com

This little place nestled in the heart of the Heights offers a fantastic steak night every Mon from 6 to 10 p.m., when $14 will get you a sixteen-ounce rib eye and baked potato. Happy hour runs from 3 to 7 p.m. and includes half-price appetizers, $3 wells, and $2 domestic beers.

The Tavern on Gray
1340 W. Gray St.
(713) 522-5152
www.thetavernongray.com

This popular bar has a lot going on, from karaoke to poker to bikini contests. But on Wed and Sun, the focus turns to one word: steak. In addition to the delicious steak and potato for $15, there's also a great happy hour daily from 3 to 8 p.m. that includes $2 pints, $6 pitchers, $3 frozen margaritas and Bellinis, and $4 Smirnoff vodkas.

DRINKS:
CHEAP BUZZ

"Here's to alcohol: the cause of,
and solution to, all of life's problems."

—HOMER SIMPSON

Oh, the joy of cocktail hour. That time in every day when you can kick back, relax, and enjoy a delicious glass of wine, a frosty mug of beer, or a girly cosmopolitan (if that's your thing). But if you're not careful, those happy hours, with-dinner drinks, and nightcaps can add up, leaving you more broke than after a night of partying with the cast of *Jersey Shore*. Fortunately, Houston has lots of ways to get a buzz on a budget. Here are some of the best tastings, happy hours, and plain ole good deals in the city.

A **LITTLE** OF **THIS**, A **LITTLE** OF **THAT**

There are few things better in life than free drinks. Instead of waiting on the guy at the end of the bar to buy them for you, why not head to places that regularly offer up free wine, cocktails, and beer to customers? Seem too good to be true? It isn't. Read on.

Block 7 Wine Company
720 Shepherd Dr.
(713) 572-2565
www.block7wineco.com

This popular wine bar is a relative newcomer to the area, but already it's making a name for itself thanks to the quality and quantity of wines it sells. It also offers frequent wine tastings that give visitors a chance to try out multiple wines—for free. All wines tasted are available for take-home purchase. Block 7 also offers a happy hour from 4 to 6 p.m. Mon through Fri that includes $4 happy hour bites and $4 drinks such as sangria, sherry, and prosecco. Bites include truffle popcorn, Vietnamese spring rolls, and smoked bacon and caramelized onion mini–flat bread.

The Dirt Bar
222 Yale St.
(713) 426-4222
www.dirtbar.com

The Catch: Your free drink is up to the flip of a coin. Call it wrong and you pay.

The Dirt Bar is one of the best little bars in town, a dark, divey little place where the music is eclectic, the drinks are solid, and the crowd is a great mix, from rock 'n' rollers to businesspeople who just got out of work. The owners even encourage local bands to drop off their CDs so they can play them at the bar. Can you say awesome? Tuesday is the legendary "flip night," when the bartender flips a coin and if you call it correctly you get your drink for free. Call it wrong? Pony up the cash, my friend. But don't be too bummed. The worst night at Dirt Bar is better than the best night at a lot of other places in Houston.

The Drinkery
4115 Washington Ave.
(713) 426-3617
www.washingtonavenuedrinkery.com

The motto here is, "We're not drunk, we're just drinking!" That pretty much sums it up. With a huge bar and a huge space, this bar has a lot of appeal for all varieties of folks. And from 4 to 7 p.m. on Wed, you can throw a ring at the bar's "mountain o' liquor," and if you hook a bottle you get a free shot, cocktail, or beer. The cost is $2 for three throws. (Oh, and if you miss, they'll still give you a Jello shot—sounds like a win-win to me). Another great deal is on Mon, when you can buy a Drinkery glass for $5 and get refills for $2 every Monday on. There's also a *Mad Men* viewing party on Sun.

Haak Vineyards and Winery
6310 Avenue T, Santa Fe
(409) 925-1401
www.haakwine.com

The Catch: Tours are $5 per person but include four tastings.

Whether you wander the long rows of grapes, enjoy a picnic on the lawn, or sip a glass from the wide outside patio, to visit Haak Vineyards and Winery is to step into a relaxed, lovely little world. But let's face it: The main reason anyone goes to a winery is for the wine, and the selection here is fabulous, from a caramelly Blanc du Bois white port, to a spicy Tempranillo, to sweet Pink Pelican blush. Stop by on the hour from 11 a.m. to 6 p.m. Mon through Fri, 11 a.m. to 7 p.m. on Sat, or noon to 5 p.m. on Sun for a tour and tasting, which includes four samples. Visitors under twenty-one may enjoy the tour (but not the tastings) for free. Want more samples? Fork over $15 for a VIP tour, which includes a logo glass and seven tastings. The winery also hosts Sunday concerts, festivals, and wine dinners. Check the website for details.

Houston Wine Merchant
2646 S. Shepherd Dr.
(713) 524-3397
www.houstonwines.com

This store, which specializes in providing fine wines to the community, is stocked with bottle after glorious bottle of some of the best vino you'll find in Houston. And even better, if you go on Fri or Sat, you can taste some of it without spending a cent. The store hosts open-house-style tastings from 5 to 7 p.m. on Fri and from 2 to 4 p.m. on Sat. The types of wine sampled change weekly, and representatives from various vineyards and wineries are often available to answer any questions. Not all that into wine? The store also sells a variety of fine liquors. The store's bimonthly newsletter is also a great resource to learn about new products and events.

Messina Hof Winery
545 Old Reliance Rd., Bryan
(979) 778-9463
www.messinahof.com

The Catch: Tours are $5 per person but include a souvenir wine glass and four tastings.

There's lots more to do at this winery than drink wine. You can dine in the on-site restaurant, drop in for a wine appreciation class, or even stay overnight at Villa at Messina Hof bed-and-breakfast. But regardless of what brings you here, you'll want to enjoy the tour and tastings, which are $5 and offered on the hour during regular business hours. For $7, you can take a private tour during business hours (minimum of ten people; advance reservations required), and for $12 you can get one after hours. Tours are approximately one hour. The tasting room is open from 10 a.m. to 7 p.m. Mon through Sat and from 11 a.m. to 6 p.m. on Sun. Tours are held at 1, 2:30, and 5:30 p.m. Mon through Fri; 11 a.m. and 12:30, 4, and 5:30 p.m. on Sat; and 12:30, 2:30, and 4 p.m. on Sun.

Nundini Italian Market and Deli

500 N. Shepherd Dr.
(713) 861-6331
www.nundini.com

You may expect to see Tony Soprano when you walk in the doors at this wide Italian market—it's *that* authentic. From creamy gelato to hand-pulled cheeses to pastas, olive oils, and meats you rarely see outside of Italy, this market is an Italian food lover's dream. And, thanks to its Friday wine tastings, it's also a wine lover's dream and a chance to taste Italian wines not widely available in the United States. The store is open from 10 a.m. to 6 p.m. daily; tastings are typically from 6 to 8 p.m. on Fri, but call ahead to check. And if you have a little time before the tasting, grab a quick panini, which are made fresh and include ingredients such as prosciutto, salmon, and roasted peppers.

Saint Arnold Brewing Company

2000 Lyons Ave.
(713) 686-9494
www.saintarnold.com

The Catch: A $7 admission fee, which includes a souvenir tasting glass, is required.

Texas's oldest craft brewery, this beloved Houston treasure recently moved into a bigger, better building. What does that mean for you? More tours and tastings, all week long. The brewery regularly produces ten beers (five are year-round, five are seasonal) that range from a hoppy India pale ale (Saint Arnold Elissa) to a full-bodied, chocolaty stout (Saint Arnold Winter Stout). Kids are also welcome at the brewery but will be limited to tasting Saint Arnold Root Beer. Guests are admitted on Sat between 11 a.m. and 2 p.m. for tours at noon, 1, and 2 p.m. After your tour, you'll receive four generous samples. On weekdays the tour is held at 3 p.m. Think you'll get hungry? Pack a lunch. Food is welcome at these tours, which have a party-like atmosphere.

Shot Bar Houston

2315 Bagby St.
(713) 526-3000
www.shotbarhouston.com

The Catch: You spin a wheel to determine your fate. You may get free shots for the whole bar or end up drinking a chocolate-cake–themed monstrosity— that you pay for—more likely to give you a sugar rush than a buzz.

The concept here is simple: Every good night includes a few rounds of shots. If you're not sure what kind of shot to order at your favorite local bar, come here, where they have a ton of options readily available. The crowd can be a bit frat-tastic and the drinks a bit overpriced, but if you land on a free shot when the bartender spins the wheel, you're set for the evening. You can also donate a shot glass from your own personal collection to the bar for decoration and score a free drink that way. Just be sure you dress to impress—the bouncers can be jerks about it.

Southern Star Brewing Company
1207 N. FM 3083 Rd. East, Conroe
(936) 441-2739
www.southernstarbrewery.com

Located inside a 10,000-square-foot warehouse, this relatively new brewery (it was founded in 2008) is turning out some popular brands, such as the Buried Hatchet and Bombshell Blonde, to distributors across Texas. But if you go directly to the source on a Saturday afternoon, you'll find you can get your hands on some of those refreshing brews without opening your wallet. The Saturday tours, which go from 1 to 3 p.m., include multiple tastings and are open to all ages. No reservations are required; barbecue is available for purchase on-site, as is merchandise. There is no climate control in the building, however, so dress appropriately for the weather.

The Tasting Room—Uptown Park
1101 Uptown Park Blvd.
(713) 993-9800
www.tastingroomwines.com

This bright, elegant tasting space includes more than 7,600 square feet filled with more than 200 wines ranging from $15 to more than $1,000 a bottle, all of which are available for retail purchase. There are also dozens of wines to try by the glass, as well as beer, nonalcoholic beverages, and food including a fantastic Sunday brunch. But if you're not sure what you're looking for, you can't beat the Saturday tastings from 2 to 5 p.m., where $6 will get you multiple tastings of some of the finest wines out there. Decide to buy a bottle? Even better. You'll get your $6 back. The Tasting Room—Uptown Park is open from 11 a.m. to midnight Mon through Fri, 11 a.m. to 1 a.m. on Sat, and 10 a.m. to 10 p.m. on Sun.

Union Bar
2708 Bagby St.
(281) 974-1916
www.unionbarhouston.com

Stumble down Bagby on a Friday night and you'll find something almost unheard of in the bar scene: an open bar. That's right, every Fri from 9 to 10 p.m. Union Bar offers an open bar. Sure, most of the liquor is well . . . , but it's FREE. Even if you miss this hallowed hour, Union Bar is worth a visit. The stripper poles that adorn the lounge are an instant conversation starter, and the other weekday specials (think $2 beers and $3 shots) make it well worth a visit.

HAPPY **HOURS**

Big Woodrow's
3111 Chimney Rock Rd.
(713) 784-2653
www.bigwoodrows.com

This place is quintessential Texas. Sprawling patios. Cheap beer. The LSU fans who stuff into the bar every fall. OK, it's actually a Cajun place, but no matter, this is a great bar with great food—especially if you go during one of the nights with specials, such as Tues, when pitchers are $7, or Thurs, when domestic pints are just a buck. The multiple TVs do make this a great place to watch a game, but my favorite nights there have been enjoyed at a picnic table, eating crawfish with friends.

Branch Water Tavern
510 Shepherd Dr.
(713) 863-7777
www.branchwatertavern.com

One of the newer "it" restaurants in Houston's culinary scene, Branch Water Tavern aims to offer "artisan American food and drink" to the town's foodie community. Menu regulars include items such as fried oyster po'boy, chicken potpie, and seared red snapper. Happy hour specials, which run from 4 to 7 p.m., include a daily whiskey beverage for $3; $2 beer; $20 wine bottles; $5 you call its; and discounted appetizers such as crispy stuffed olives ($4), duck-fat popcorn ($3), and oysters on the half shell ($1 each).

Brian O'Neill's Irish Pub
5555 Morningside Dr.
(713) 522-2603
www.brianoneills.com

If you like happy hour (and, let's face it, who *doesn't* like happy hour?), this one is a can't miss, with specials for every type of drinker out there. Held from 3 to 9 p.m. Tues through Sat and 11 a.m. to 2 a.m. Sun through Mon, happy hour here includes $1.75 well drinks, $2.00 house wine, $2.00 twenty-ounce domestic drafts, $2.25 twenty-ounce Shiner drafts, $6.00 domestic pitchers, $7.00 Shiner pitchers, and $7.00 Amstel Light pitchers. Daily specials include $10.00 pizza and domestic pitchers on Mon, half-price shepherd's pie on Tues, half-price burgers on Wed, steak night on Sat, and brunch and half-price fish-and-chips on Sun.

Brixx Houston
5110 Washington Ave.
(713) 864-8811
www.brixxhouston.com

You have to expect a certain amount of too-cool-for-school clientele and some occasionally aloof bartenders here, but you might be pleasantly surprised by the deals you can find. For example, on the Thursday ladies' night at this Washington Avenue establishment, you can score $5 Tommy Bahama rum drinks and $7 Grey Goose products from 9 p.m. to closing time. On Sun, get ready for all-you-can-eat crawfish, $3 domestic pints, and $9 domestic pitchers (be warned, though—there's a DJ on Sun, and the scene can get quite loud). Still, it's worth the trip for the deals and the ample outside seating.

Get Your Grub On

With all the money you'll be saving on cheap drinks, you might as well treat yourself to some delicious food. Here are five places that up the ante when it comes to pub fare.

The Black Labrador

4100 Montrose Blvd.

(713) 529-1199

www.blacklabradorpub.com

From the giant chessboard out front to the cozy atmosphere inside, this place couldn't be more welcoming. Even more welcoming is its classic British pub grub, which includes a ploughman's lunch of cheeses, bread, and pickled onions; steak and kidney pie that includes beef, veal, mushrooms, onions, and spices; and scotched beef that mixes beef and fresh vegetables in a Guinness stock with herbs. Not into British food? Salads, soups, and sandwiches are also available. Lunch and dinner is offered daily, and Sunday brunch starts at 11 a.m.

BRC

519 Shepherd Dr.

(713) 861-2233

www.brcgastropub.com

Although it's pretty new to the scene, this gastro pub is already making a splash. The most obvious feature is its name—BRC stands for Big Red Cock, a tribute to the giant red rooster that stands outside the restaurant as its mascot. Less obvious but just as important is this pub's fantastic food, which includes Dr Pepper Fried San Antonio Quail, blue crab beignets, and mussels and fries. Don't miss the sides here, either, which include sautéed garlicky spinach, blue cheese potato salad, and fresh-baked bacon-cheddar biscuits. If you sit at the bar, consider grabbing one of the fresh-baked pretzels you'll see propped up with the pretzel stands on the counter.

Brick House Tavern

12910 Northwest Freeway

(713) 462-0576

www.brickhousetavernandtap.com

The first time I walked in here, I was shocked—not by the menu, but by the girls in crop tops and tiny jean shorts who were waiting on me. I looked at the sign. Had I accidentally stumbled into Hooters? But then I looked at the menu, which looked so good that I said, "Oh hell, I'll just stay." I'm glad I did. Regardless of the atmosphere, the food here is top notch, ranging from pub standards such as chicken tenders and soft pretzels (the best soft pretzels I've had, served with queso, regular mustard, and honey mustard) to more eclectic fare such as a wedge salad, barbecued baby-back ribs, and steak and eggs. The full bar and extensive beer list don't hurt, either.

Goose's Acre Bistro and Irish Pub

21 Waterway Ave., The Woodlands
(281) 466-1502
www.thegoosesacre.com

It may be a trek to get there, but if you're heading to The Woodlands for a concert or some shopping, don't miss this authentic Irish restaurant and bar originally from Midleton, Ireland. When the bar was forced to close in 2005, owners Brian Young and Colm O'Neill moved it—piece by piece, almost—to Texas. The menu includes basic Irish favorites such as codfish and chips, corned beef and cabbage, and sirloin shepherd's pie, as well as American faves such as fried mozzarella, build-your-own pizza, and barbecued beef-back ribs.

Kenneally's Irish Pub

2111 S. Shepherd Dr.
(713) 630-0486
www.irishpubkenneallys.com

This small Irish pub is St. Patrick's Day central every March. But a little known fact about this great little bar is that it turns out some delicious Chicago-style pizza. Made from scratch, this thin-crust pizza comes with various toppings including corned beef, jalapeños, anchovies, fresh tomatoes, and more. Other food, such as homemade potato chips, Irish nachos, and a cheeseburger platter, are also available. The bar is open from 3 p.m. to 2 a.m. Tues through Sun and 4 p.m. to 2 a.m. on Mon. The kitchen is open from 3 p.m. to 1 a.m. Mon through Sat and from 3 to 11 p.m. on Sun.

Cedar Creek Cafe

1034 W. 20th St.
(713) 808-9623
http://cedarcreek.squarespace.com

If you're a fan of Crown Royal, you won't want to miss Mondays at this fun little joint known for its delicious menu offerings and laid-back vibe. That's because on Monday, $5 will get you Crown all day long. Other Monday specials include 50 cent wings, $10 for a burger and a domestic pint, $7 domestic pitchers, and $12 buckets of Bud Light, Budweiser, and Bud Light Lime. Other weekly specials include discounts on Texas beers every Tues, Sweet Tea vodka specials on Wed, $4 Three Olives products on Thurs, and $4 frozen drinks on Fri. Happy hour is from 4 to 7 p.m. daily. Cedar Creek is open from 10 a.m. to midnight Mon through Wed, 10 a.m. to 2 a.m. Thurs through Fri, 7 a.m. to 2 a.m. on Sat, and 7 a.m. to midnight on Sun.

Christian's Tailgate

2000 Bagby St.
(713) 527-0261
www.christianstailgate.com

If you've lived in Houston long, chances are good that you've heard of Christian's Tailgate. It's got a nationally known hamburger, it used to have a locally known arm-wrestling competition, and it now offers one of the most solid happy hours in the city. Here's a sample: Monday is Greek night, with $1 drafts and $4 pitchers (with student ID) and a free beer pong tournament at 8:30 p.m. With a $30 bar tab payment for first place, you may even make money on this deal. Other weekly specials include $1 drafts and $2 wells from 9 p.m. to 2 a.m. on Wed and $2 wells, $2 beer, $2 Crown Royal, and $2 Jack Daniels for ladies on Thurs (as well as karaoke). Oh, and football fans: This is a great place (with great specials) to watch the game.

Darkhorse Tavern

2207 Washington Ave.
(713) 426-2442
www.dhtavern.com

This cool little neighborhood bar is housed in a building from the 1920s and keeps that vibe with its pressed tin ceilings, oak bar, and mica lamps. It offers happy hour from 4 to 7 p.m. daily; specials include $3.00 Jager on

Mon; $3.50 premium pints on Tues; happy hour until 11 p.m. on Wed; $5.00 single malt scotch on Thurs; and $3.50 Bloody Marys on Sun. If the weather is nice, grab a spot on the patio. The bar is open from 4 p.m. to 2 a.m. Mon through Sat and 2 p.m. to 2 a.m. on Sun.

Firkin & Phoenix
1915 Westheimer Rd.
(713) 526-3100
www.firkinandphoenix.com

This is a bar's bar: good pub grub, good crowd, good drink specials—particularly during happy hour from 2 to 7 p.m. Mon through Fri, when domestic beers are $2.50, imports are $3.50, and wells are $3.50. Other weekly discounts include free pool, trivia night, and $8.00 fried chicken on Mon; 40 cent wings and $3.00 twenty-three-ounce beer on Tues; $8.00 Miller Lite pitchers on Wed; $2.50 select domestic pints on Thurs; shot specials on Fri; and $3.00 Bloody Marys, Bellinis, and mimosas all day on Sat and Sun.

Flying Saucer
705 Main St.
(713) 228-9472
www.beerknurd.com

Another favorite of businessmen and women who work downtown, the Flying Saucer is a beer lover's dream (with a full bar for those who aren't). With 240 beers and 100 styles of beer, it won't be hard to find something you like. And with happy hour specials from 4 to 7 p.m. Mon through Thurs and 4 to 8 p.m. on Fri, it won't be hard to have a taste or two without breaking your budget. For example, on Mon, you can grab one of more than seventy-five draft beers for just $3. For a real taste of the regulars, go on Tues, when the bar is packed for trivia night. If you're not picky, order one of the "Fire Sale" beverages listed on the chalkboard by the bar. At just $3 or so, you'll be drinking great beer—for cheap. The menu here is solid, too. The bar is open 11 a.m. to 1 a.m. Mon through Wed, 11 a.m. to 2 a.m. Thurs through Fri, noon to 2 a.m. on Sat, and noon to midnight on Sun.

House of Blues Houston
1204 Caroline St.
(713) 652-5837
www.houseofblues.com

Heading to House of Blues Houston for a concert? Even if you're not, it's worth stopping by this music-loving chain's downstairs bar for the fabulous happy hour held Mon through Fri from 4 to 7 p.m. Specials include $2 domestic beer bottles, $3 imported beer bottles, and $4 house wines and house cocktails. All appetizers are also half price during this time.

Kelvin Arms
2424 Dunstan Rd.
(713) 528-4739

The only Scottish pub in Houston, Kelvin Arms opened in 2000 and has drawn a consistent crowd of followers thanks to its cool layout (one of the rooms is an old bank vault), its freebies (including darts and popcorn all day, every day), and its stiff drinks. During happy hour, which runs daily from 3 to 7 p.m., this fun little place gets even more appealing thanks to $3 wells and $1 off all draft beers. The staff here can be a little questionable—I've had my songs on the jukebox skipped on numerous occasions, and I can assure you I wasn't playing anything nearly as offensive as the Britney Spears–sounding number I heard last time I was there), but overall it's a great place to spend a few hours.

Kobain
3720 Raymond St.
(713) 862-9911
www.kobain.net

By attempting to draw rock music fans who will appreciate its attention to '70s, '80s, and indie rock, Kobain has created for itself an odd mix of regulars. Some come to be seen, while others come simply to listen. Something they both can agree on, however, is happy hour, which is daily from 4 to 8 p.m. Specials include $2 domestics, $4 shot specials, and half-price appetizers on Mon and Tues; $13 steak and potato, $5 bombs, and $4 wine on Wed; half off champagne splits and bottles on Thurs; and a full brunch menu with $10 mimosa specials until 4 p.m. on Sun.

Komodo Pub
2004 Baldwin St.
(713) 655-1501

Admittedly, it can take a few trips to warm up to this bar, which is located inside a house in the trendy Midtown district. But once you get used to the shabby chic decor, you'll find it as comfortable as grandma's house for Sunday dinner, except that the order of the day is a cocktail instead of chicken. While the Midtown scene can be overpriced, this place offers a great happy hour from 2 to 8 p.m. Mon through Sat that includes wells and some beers for $2.75. They also have an extensive shot list (ask for the "nuclear rainbow") and offer generous wine tastings for $10 on Wed. Overall, the pub offers some great deals in a really charming place. Oh, and did I mention the drinks are particularly stiff? They are.

The Lot
4212 Washington Ave.
(713) 868-5688
www.thelothouston.net

Yet another Washington bar with great deals, the Lot is a relative newcomer that packs a solid punch. Expect to find specials most nights that may include $2.50 mimosas, $5.00 Jack and ginger ale, and $15 domestic buckets (Sun); $2 drafts and $4 Jager (Tues); $5 Ketel One (Wed); $2 domestic bottles and $4 sweet tea drinks (Thurs), and more. The bar is also fond of special events, such as a reverse happy hour with $2 drafts and champagne specials and even a late-night "cougar power hour" (don't ask).

McCormick and Schmick's
1151 Uptown Park Blvd.
(713) 840-7900
www.mccormickandschmicks.com

The happy hour food menu here is known for having solid, and very affordable, fare. But the drink menu during happy hour is just as good, with everything from sangria to martinis to beer and wine. Some recent specialties have included $3.95 ZiegenBock drafts, $3.95 chilled Gekkeikan sake, $4.95 lemon drop cocktails, $4.95 "perfect peach" fuzzy navels, $6.95 Cruzan tropical rum punch, $6.95 Ultimat raspberry cosmopolitan, $5.95 Canyon Road cabernet, and $5.95 Canyon Road chardonnay. On Thurs, it's martini night with $5.95 cosmos, martinis, and appletinis. Happy hour is held from 4 to 7 p.m. Mon through Fri. There is a minimum $3.50 beverage purchase per person. Additional locations are at 1201 Fannin St. (713-658-8100) and 791 Town & Country Blvd. (713-465-3685).

McElroys Irish Pub
3607 S. Sandman
(713) 524-2444
www.mcelroyspub.com

Expect good drinks and friendly folks when you visit this Irish pub, which is nestled into a corner near Houston's Museum District. The place is pretty small and basic, but what it's lacking in atmosphere is made up for with drink specials. The daily happy hour runs from 3 to 8 p.m., and daily drink specials are also offered. A sampling includes $2.50 Lone Star bottles every day; $3.00 Shiner pints on Mon; $3.75 Blue Moon pints on Tues; $4.00 Guinness on Wed; $1.00 off import bottles on Thurs; $4.00 Harp and Smithwicks on Fri; $4.00 Saint Arnold pints on Sat, and $2.75 Miller Lite and Bud Light pints on Sun. McElroys is open daily from 3 p.m. to 2 a.m.

Pearl Bar
4216 Washington Ave.
(713) 868-5337
www.thepearlbarhouston.com

Another member of the trendy Washington elite, this bar has managed to keep a great happy hour that includes $1.50 drafts and $2.00 wells. Other weekly events include a twenty-three-ounce Pearl pilsner for $8.00 (you keep the glass), and $4.00 you call its on Wed. Be warned, however: On weekends the bar turns into a scene, with a DJ blasting '80s and '90s music, and guys and girls dressed to the nines.

Poison Girl
1641 Westheimer Rd.
(713) 527-9929
www.myspace.com/poisongirlbar

It may predominantly be a hipster hangout, but this dive bar located alongside Westheimer's antiques and secondhand shops has plenty of draws for Joe Schmoe beer drinker. For one, there's the gigantic Cabbage Patch kid out back that's a great conversation topic/photo op. But even better are the drink specials. Find $2 Lone Stars, $3 Shiner drafts, and $3 shots of Jager all day, every day. And during happy hour from 5 to 8 p.m., look for $2.00 wells and $2.50 drafts.

Pub Fiction
2303 Smith St.
(713) 400-8400
www.pubfiction.com

For several years now this has been one of the trendiest bars in Midtown, and with good reason. It's got a wide variety of drinks, a fun atmosphere, and great live music. And if you go during happy hour, you'll get to feel out the entire scene—for about half the price. Held weekdays from 4 to 8 p.m., this happy hour includes $6 domestic pitchers, $2 domestic pints and $3 imported pints, and $4 vodka drinks and martinis. Daily specials include $3.00 Mexican bottled beer and $3.00 Jager and Tuaca shots all night on Mon; twenty-five-ounce domestic drafts for $3.00 and imported drafts for $4.00 on Tues; $10.00 domestic buckets and 35 cent wings on Wed; $4.00 Jim Beam and $2.00 Lone Star and PBR cans all night on Thurs; half-price wine and imported drafts as well as $2.00 wells, $2.50 mimosas, and $3.00 Bloody Marys on Sat; and $3.50 twenty-five-ounce domestic drafts, $4.50 twenty-five-ounce imported drafts, $3.00 Bloody Marys, $1.50 mimosas, and $3.00 frozen drinks on Sun. A half-price chef's menu is also offered on Mon and Tues.

Red Lion Pub
2316 S. Shepherd Dr.
(713) 782-3030
www.redlionhouston.com

Between the darts, the traditional British fare, the outside seating, and the national attention (including an appearance on Guy Fieri's *Diners, Drive-Ins and Dives*), this place doesn't really need any extra press. But the fact of the matter is that it deserves it because it's such as fun place to go. And it's even better during happy hour, when beers are $1 off and certain wines are also on special. Go for an hour, but be prepared—you might just stay for a night.

Richmond Arms Pub
5920 Richmond Ave.
(713) 784-7722
www.richmondarmsonline.com

Another favorite spot for British pub lovers, the Richmond Arms offers a nice diversion from the usual Washington and Midtown scenes. And with a weekday happy hour from 4 to 7 p.m. that includes domestic drafts for

If You Want to Splurge a Little . . .

They may not be as known for their specials, but these three can't-miss drinking spots are also worth a visit.

Anvil Bar & Refuge
1424 Westheimer Rd.
(713) 523-1622
www.anvilhouston.com
OK, so it's not the cheapest place in Houston, but its got more buzz surrounding it than any cocktail lounge that's opened in the past ten years. Why? Because of its forward-thinking attitude toward cocktails that includes using items such as house-made bitters, fresh ingredients, and hard-to-find liqueurs. Even the layout is thoughtfully designed, from the bar's foot rail, made from a freight rail track forged in the 1950s, to reclaimed meat-locker doors that lead to the restrooms and kitchen. No, it's not particularly cheap, but it's a must-try-once place to go. Menu favorites include the blueberry smash (white rum, local blueberries, and lemon; $8), the Brave (Mezcal, Curacao, Angostura bitters, and other ingredients; $12), and a Local Peach Sour (peach-infused bourbon, lemon, turbinado, egg white, and Angostura bitters; $10), as well as a full range of classic cocktails. The bar is open daily from 5 p.m. to 2 a.m.; Sunday brunch starts at 11 a.m.

Beaver's
2310 Decatur St.
(713) 864-2328
www.beavershouston.com
This restaurant-bar is constantly making waves for its innovative (and delicious) takes on cocktails. By placing an emphasis on local ingre-

dients while keeping a penchant for the unexpected, Beaver's has a way of surprising you with what it has up its sleeve. Recent "dam good cocktails" (get it?) have included the Black Mission Cup (Pimms No. 1 gin, Texas figs, lemon, Angostura bitters; $8), the Belt Strap (Cruzan Black Strap Rum, Southern Star Pine Belt Ale, and sugar and lemon; $8), and the Yellow Daisy (a house margarita made from Siembra Azul organic tequila, Yellow Chartreuse, lime, and orange blossom water; $9). Also impressive is the beer list and happy hour, with select $6 cocktails, $5 glasses of trash can punch, and $10 buckets of Lone Star and PBR.

Under the Volcano
2349 Bissonnet St.
(713) 526-5282
www.underthevolcanohouston.com
Everything about this place is solid: the delicious food, the fun drinks, and the cool name, taken from the Malcolm Lowry novel of the same title. The cocktails here are top notch, ranging from a fantastic Bloody Mary originally from Paris that's so filling it will take the place of dinner to a rum-and-lemon creation that incorporates the lychee nut. Standouts include the strawberry basil margarita (you'd be surprised by the cool kick the basil adds to the mix), the whiskey smash, and, my favorite, the frozen screwdriver, which drinks like Slurpee but will hit you like a shot. Need something to soak up all that alcohol? Check out the food menu, which includes fare such as brie with raspberry chipotle sauce, edamame, house-smoked salmon, a chimichurri roast beef sandwich, and Italian queso with sautéed eggplant, tomatoes, bell peppers, olives, and capers with hot melted cheese and tortilla chips.

$2.50, pitchers for $7.50, and well drinks for $4.50, there's really not much to dislike. Daily specials include $1.00 off martinis on Mon, $2.75 Miller Lite from noon to 7 p.m. on Sat, and $2.75 Miller Lite bottles and domestic drafts from 2 p.m. to 2 a.m. on Sun. The food here is solid as well.

Salt Bar
4216 Washington Ave.
(713) 868-5155
www.saltbarhouston.com

We Texans know our margaritas. So when I heard about Salt Bar, a margarita-themed bar that just opened in the Washington Corridor, I was intrigued. And once I heard about their happy hour specials, I was impressed. The bar's happy hour is offered daily until 8 p.m. (impressive, given the typical 6 or 7 p.m. ending times) and includes $3 frozen margaritas, $3 pints, $3 wells, and bottomless chips and salsa. Nightly specials include $4 frozen margaritas and $2 toppers all day long on Mon; beer with a shot of Cazadores Silver for $8 and house margarita pitchers for $15 on Tues; $5 Cabo Wobblys all night on Wed; frozen margaritas for $4 all night on Thurs; and bottomless frozen margaritas and chips and salsa for $25 on Sun.

Sambuca
909 Texas St.
(713) 224-5299
www.sambucarestaurant.com

This sexy little spot located in the heart of downtown is known for its live music and lunch specials, but it also has a happy hour that's well worth a trip all by itself. Every weekday from 4:30 to 6:30 p.m., Sambuca offers half-price wells and call drinks, as well as half-price appetizers and pizza.

Sawyer Park
2412 Washington Ave.
(713) 863-9350
www.sawyerparkhouston.com

Located on the always-hopping Washington Corridor, Sawyer Park is well suited for any kind of crowd, from sports lovers who come for its big screens to club-goers who visit for the weekend DJs. But if you want a bargain, you need to go between 4 and 9 p.m. on weekdays, when domestic drafts are

$2.50 and all other drinks are $1.00 off. Other weekday specials include $3.00 Three Olive vodka drinks on Mon, bingo on Tues, 25 cent wings and $2.50 Saint Arnold drafts and bottles on Wed, $2.00 Mexican beer and $3.00 Cazadores shots on Thurs, and $10.00 domestic pitchers on Sat.

Shuck Daddy's
1511 Shepherd Dr.
(713) 861-9888
www.shuckdaddys.com

OK, so the theme here is oysters, and there are indeed lots of different types. But if you really want to have a good time, time your visit with happy hour, which runs from 3 to 7 p.m. Mon through Sat and includes $2.25 domestic longnecks, $3.00 wells, $4.00 calls, and $5.00 premiums. Food specials include 50 cent oysters and $2.50 tacos. Grab a seat at a picnic table out back and enjoy the breeze as you sip on your super-cheap suds.

Smith & Wollensky
4007 Westheimer Rd.
(713) 621-7555
www.smithandwollensky.com

This regional chain's bar is packed on weeknights, and that's with good reason: Their happy hour menu is a can't lose. It's packed with fresh food and solid drink specials, and you'll want to pull up a seat at the bar, too. Drink specials include Shiner and Miller Lite bottles for $4, house wines for $4, Absolut martinis for $7, and a fun "prickly 'rita" for $7. Happy hour is held from 4 to 7 p.m. Food options include $6 flat breads, $9 fried calamari, $7 fried shrimp, $6 spicy fries, and $8 mini crab cakes. Just don't get so focused on your food and drinks that you forget to look around; the people-watching here is spectacular.

Sonoma Retail Wine Bar & Restaurant
2720 Richmond Ave.
(713) 526-9463
www.sonomahouston.com

Don't want to travel to a winery to get that laid-back vineyard vibe? Head to Sonoma Retail Wine Bar & Restaurant, an upscale winery-themed lounge in Houston's Upper Kirby area that offers a solid happy hour with some of the best wines in the country. Sure, happy hour here means $7 to $10 a glass, but if you know a bit about wine you'll understand why this is such a good deal the minute you see the wine list. Wine flights and an extensive beer list are also available, and wine classes are available by appointment. Oh, and if you get hungry, be sure to check out the restaurant's menu, which includes hand-rolled gourmet pizza, sliders, small plates of risotto, scallops, and crostini, as well as salads, cheeses, and charcuterie.

Taco Milagro
2555 Kirby Dr.
(713) 522-1999
www.taco-milagro.com

Long a place to see and be seen, this popular restaurant is known for great drinks, delicious food, and good-looking clientele. But every weekday from 4 to 7 p.m., it also becomes a bargain hunter's paradise thanks to impressive drink specials such as $3.50 margaritas and $1.00 off beers. There are also $1.99 fish tacos all day Mon and $10.00 bottles of wine on Wed, as well as salsa dancing starting at 7 p.m.

Voice Lounge
220 Main St.
(713) 224-4266
www.hotelicon.com

This gorgeous bar-restaurant is nestled inside one of Houston's favorite boutique hotels in the heart of downtown. And on Wednesday, they bring their A game with $1 well martinis from 4 to 7 p.m. That's right, $1. Can't make it on Wednesday? Try mussels and a glass of wine for $8.50 on Mon, a burger and a beer with sides for $10.00 on Tues, and $3.00 drafts, $4.00 wells, and $5.00 wines on Fri.

SPECIAL **DAY,** CHEAP **DRINKS**

When you want to find a great deal, half of the challenge is knowing the right time to go. Instead of limiting themselves to happy hour, these places also offer specials on certain days of the week. You'll want to mark your calendar with these daily specials.

Cecil's Tavern
600 W. Gray St.
(713) 524-3691

The inside of this tavern is dark and moody with a jukebox that frequently plays bands such as the Beastie Boys, Rage Against the Machine, and Faith No More. Outside is a large, comfortable patio. It's a nice place to get a beer any night, but no night is better than Monday, when Lone Stars are $1, as are house well drinks. Can you beat that? Probably not. There are other drink specials throughout the week, and grilled tacos on certain nights. Call for details.

Cova Hand-Selected Wines
5600 Kirby Dr.
(713) 838-0700
www.covawines.com

Sure, a good wine is worth its weight in grapes, but why pay full price for a glass of vino when you could get it for half off? Head to Cova Hand-Selected Wines on Saturday night and you'll get 50 percent off any glass of wine on the "Wine by the Glass List" from a bottle that has already been opened. There are fifty bottles on this list, so you're likely to find something good. Can't make it Saturday? Head over during happy hour from 4 to 7 p.m. Mon through Fri, when select wines are $5 and tapas are $7.

Front Porch Pub
217 Gray St.
(713) 571-9571
www.frontporchpub.com

Right in the heart of Midtown, this fun bar is popular among the twenty-something set for its big TVs, wide outside deck, and delicious drinks. If you go on Monday, you'll find a great deal with $2 pints of domestic light beer after 5 p.m. Wings are also 25 cents on Monday. The menu here is also a standout, featuring everything from baked pretzels to Philly cheesesteaks (served with your choice of fries or chips and salsa, naturally) to a veggie-melt sandwich. There's trivia every Tues and steak night on Thurs.

The Ginger Man

5607 Morningside Dr.
(713) 526-2770
www.houston.gingermanpub.com

Known as one of the best beer bars in Houston, the Ginger Man serves well over a hundred beers from everywhere from China to Jamaica. With its dartboards and jukebox, the inside is inviting, and the large beer garden in the back is the perfect place to spend a nice afternoon. Even better are the specials, which take place nearly every night of the week. My favorites are Spaten Sundays, when all Spaten drafts are $3.50 a pint, and Texas Thursdays, when all draft Texas beers are $1.00 off all day. The bar also regularly offers tastings; check the website for details. Wine and ciders are also available here.

The Harp

1625 Richmond Ave.
(713) 528-7827
www.theharphouston.com

If you're the type who likes a good game of trivia, The Harp is one of your best bets. The pub, which proudly calls itself "Houston's friendliest Irish pub," has a great trivia night each week that includes $2.50 Bud Light draft, free pizza, and the self-proclaimed best-looking trivia crowd in town. Trivia night is held from 8 to 10:30 p.m. every Tues; the cost is $3 per person with teams of up to five people. The bar is open from 3 p.m. to 2 a.m. Mon through Fri and 4 p.m. to 2 a.m. Sat through Sun.

Hotel ZaZa

5701 Main St.
(713) 526-1991
www.hotelzazahouston.com

This is one of the swankiest hotels in Houston, but thankfully for us, its famous Monarch Bistro and Lounge offers a bunch of deals that will make even the biggest tightwad feel right at home. One of the most notable is the restaurant's new "neighborhood night," an all-night happy hour starting at 5 p.m. on Thurs that includes $5 beer, wine, well drinks, and appetizers. On Wed, dinner is half off at Monarch, and on Mon, bottles of wine are half price.

Little Woodrow's

5611 Morningside Dr.
(713) 521-2337
www.littlewoodrows.com

This little ice house is popular among the area's students and young professionals for its diverse jukebox, ample outside seating, and cheap beer. At no time is their attention to cheap beer more obvious than on Thurs, when twenty-five-ounce "giant mugs" are just $4. Other weekly specials include $3.00 Texas and Mexican beers (bottles and drafts) on Mon, "big ass" twenty-three-ounce beers for $2.00 to $4.00 on Tues, and $3.25 frozen margaritas, mimosas, and Dos Equis on Sat until 7 p.m. Happy hour is held from 3 to 7 p.m. daily; Lone Star pints are always $2.25. Additional locations are at 4235 Bellaire Blvd. (713-661-5282) and 2306 Brazos St. (713-522-1041).

Lucky's Pub

801 St. Emanuel
(713) 522-2010
www.luckyspub.com

Under normal circumstances, a six-ounce "small ass" beer may not be your drink of choice. But on Tuesday at Lucky's Pub, this small-ass beer is just 50 cents, meaning you can get a lot of them, all night long, for just a few Benjamins. Other Tuesday specials include $3 and $4 shots, $4 twenty-four-ounce Mexican beers, and free pool, darts, washers, and more. Daily happy hour, which is held from 4 to 7 p.m. Mon through Fri, includes $2 domestic drafts, $2 wells, and $2 wine. Other can't-miss days to visit include Fri, with a half-price selected beer and shot; Sat, with $2 Bud Light pints and $15 beer buckets; and Sun, with $2 canned beer, $3 Bloody Marys, $6 mimosa and Bellini pitchers, and $8 screwdriver pitchers.

Rainbow Lodge

2011 Ella Blvd.
(713) 861-8666
www.rainbow-lodge.com

This is one of the most famous high-end restaurants in Houston, known for its lovely views, cozy fireplaces, and regional, rustic food. But even though it may be a classy joint, it also knows how to offer a great deal, with 99 cent mimosas and champagne every Sun until 3 p.m. Want to stay past 3 p.m.?

No worries. Half-priced wine night begins at 5 p.m., when casual "Sunday suppers" filled with comfort food take over the menu.

Rudyard's British Pub

2010 Waugh Dr.
(713) 521-0521
http://rudyards.s425.sureserver.com

Even if you've never been to Rudyard's British Pub, chances are good you have a set of friends who like to hang out here. That's because this comfortable spot serves up some of the best drink specials in town, including $3.25 well drinks and $2.50 Lone Stars, Pearl beer, and Schlitz all day, every day. Other weekly specials include $3 Shiners and Rolling Rock Mon through Thurs, $1 sixteen-ounce beers, and $1 kamikazes all day Sun. Happy hour is held every day from 4 to 7 p.m., with 50 cents off most drafts and liquor. There are also free wings on Mon starting at 6 p.m. and beer tastings on the last Thurs of every month (reservations required).

Sam Houston Race Park

7575 N. Sam Houston Parkway West
(281) 807-7223
www.shrp.com

Every Houstonian should visit this park, which features live quarter-horse racing, frequent concerts, and lots of special events. But if you like beer, you'll want to visit on Friday night, when draft beer is just 50 cents and wine is $1.50 between 7 and 10 p.m. That's right—a buck will score you two beers and simulcast racing. Don't miss it.

Stag's Head Pub

2128 Portsmouth St.
(713) 533-1199
www.stagsheadpub.com

If you really want to get your money's worth (as well as a full stomach), head to the Stag's Head Pub on Tues for $5.75 domestic pitchers and $5.00 pizzas. This great little pub may serve up delicious fare such as bangers and mash, a ploughman's lunch, and fish-and-chips, but they also make one heck of a pizza. Wash it down with a pitcher and you'll be set for the night. Other nightly specials include $5.75 pitchers and half-price wings on Mon;

$3.75 Shock Top pints, $10.00 Saint Arnold's pitchers, and $12.95 steak night on Wed; $6.75 pitchers and $4.00 shots on Thurs; $9.75 Dos Equis pitchers and $7.75 Shiner pitchers on Fri and Sat; and $3.75 pints and $5.75 Shiner pitchers on Sun. Lone Star bottles are $2.50 daily after 4 p.m.

Tipsy Clover
2416 Brazos
(713) 524-0782
www.tipsyclover.com

You wouldn't expect a bar in the heart of the popular Midtown district to offer great specials, but this one does. Some of my favorites include happy hour prices and free pool all night on Sun and Mon (as well as free hot dogs and nachos during football season), $1 drafts on Tues, $3 you call its on Wed, $1 wells from 8 to 10 p.m. and shot specials all night on Thurs, and shot specials all night on Fri and Sat. The great music, outside patio, and friendly staff here add to the inviting (and cheap) atmosphere.

The Usual Pub
5519 Allen St.
(281) 501-1478
www.theusualpub.com

What'll ya have? Oh, the usual. When you come to this quaint pub, you may just decide to make this your usual hangout. After all, the drink specials are tough to beat. Weekly specials include $2.00 wells all day and $2.50 domestics from 6 to 10 p.m. on Mon; $1.00 Lone Star all day, $2.50 domestics, and $3.00 wells from 4 to 10 p.m. on Tues; $2.50 domestics and $3.00 wells from 4 to 10 p.m. on Wed; $2.50 domestics and $3.00 wells from 4 to 10 p.m. as well as karaoke on Thurs; and $2.50 domestics and $3.00 wells from 4 to 10 p.m. on Fri.

Valhalla
6100 Main St.
(713) 348-3258
www.valhalla.rice.edu

This Rice University institution has got to be one of the most interesting bars in town. First of all, it's hidden in a location so nondescript that you'd never find it unless you were looking for it. Second, all of the bartenders are volunteers, one way that the owners have found to keep costs low. And third, the drinks here are dirt cheap. What does this mean to the average visitor? A fun place with a super-smart and entertaining clientele and drinks for less than a buck. That's right: twelve-ounce Lone Star drafts here are just 95 cents. Other drafts and bottled beers, wines, and ciders are also available, as are sandwiches at lunch. Valhalla is open from 11:30 a.m. to 1 p.m. and 4 p.m. to 2 a.m. Mon through Fri and 7 p.m. to 2 a.m. on Sun; it is closed on Sat.

BEAUTY SERVICES:
CHEAP IS IN THE EYE
OF THE BEHOLDER

*"The problem with beauty is that it's like
being born rich and getting poorer."*

—JOAN COLLINS

A great massage; a fabulous haircut; a perfect new lipstick. There's something about getting a really great beauty service that can make you feel like a million bucks. But when it costs a million bucks, you've got bigger problems than the fact that your roots are showing. Thankfully, with so many beauty schools, masseuses, and salons in Houston, there are lots of options for scoring a great deal on such services.

DISCOUNT **MASSAGE** SERVICES

Avalon School of Massage
2990 Richmond Ave., Suite 200
(713) 333-5250
www.avalonmassageschool.com

This school provides discounted intern massages, but the offerings here are a bit broader than at other schools. In addition to an hour-long Swedish massage for $35, you can also schedule an hour-and-a-half-long Thai massage for $50 or a corporate chair massage at your office for $75 an hour. Couples and group massages and gift certificates are also available.

Houston School of Massage
10600 Northwest Freeway, Suite 202
(713) 681-5275
www.houstonschoolofmassage.com

Been craving a good back rub? If you schedule an appointment with the Houston School of Massage, you can score an hour-long Swedish massage for just $30. Why's it so cheap? Because it's with a student intern. Before that scares you off, though, you should know that student interns must have completed at least 250 hours of course work to give public massages, including lots of one-on-one experience with classmates and instructors. Plus, they need the hours to achieve their dreams of doing this professionally. It's almost like you're doing them a favor by getting a massage. Almost. Massages are available from 9:30 a.m. to 8:30 p.m. Mon through Fri and 9:30 a.m. to 8:30 p.m. on Sat; closed on Sun. Gift cards are also available.

Silicone City

While we're talking about beauty, I would be remiss if I didn't take a minute to point out the fact that the silicone breast implant was invented by Dr. Thomas Cronin and Dr. Frank Gerow in 1962 in, you guessed it, Houston. In 1995 *Texas Monthly* magazine wrote an article dubbing Houston "Silicone City," a nickname that stuck even though the U.S. Food and Drug Administration (FDA) had banned the implants three years earlier because of safety concerns.

Silicone implants are legal again thanks to a 2006 FDA ruling approving them in limited situations, and Houston continues to rank second only to Los Angeles in the number of breast augmentation procedures it performs every year. Sticking with the theme, here are the top five surgical cosmetic procedures performed in 2009, according to the American Society of Plastic Surgeons.

1. Breast augmentation
2. Nose reshaping
3. Eyelid surgery
4. Liposuction
5. Tummy tuck

Massage Envy

Nearly a dozen locations in the Houston area
(713) 686-3689
www.massageenvy.com

These chain massage shops have been popping up all over Houston in recent years, and for good reason. They've got a formula for massages that works. And if you're a Massage Envy newbie, you can experience their facility for just $39. Want more services than just a massage? Massage Envy is also now offering various types of facials.

Memorial Hermann Wellness Center Massage and Spa Therapy School

7731 Southwest Freeway
(713) 456-8116
www.memorialhermann.org

No matter what length of Swedish massage you're after, you can find it here, where it will be performed by a student intern who has completed core curriculum at the Memorial Hermann Wellness Center Massage and Spa Therapy School. Just want a quick, thirty-minute pick-me-up? It'll be $20. Want an hour? Just $29. Ninety minutes is $49 and two hours is $55—all much cheaper than you'd find at the average Houston salon.

Phoenix Massage Therapy School
6600 Harwin Dr., Suite 101
(713) 974-5976
www.themassageschool.com/clinic.htm

Get an hour-long massage from a student intern for $35, or buy a package of four massages and get one free (it works out to $28 per massage). Not feeling the whole massage scene? You can also opt to try a spa treatment at the on-site Tranquil Waters Day Spa, which offers lower prices than most of the other spas in the area. Packages are also available. A second campus location is at 2611 FM 1960 West. Call (281) 895-0046 for info on that branch.

Texas School of Massage
11511 Katy Freeway
(281) 531-1060
http://texasschoolofmassage.com

The motto here is "excellence in bodywork," and if you're willing to drive a little outside of town (both locations are about twenty minutes from downtown) you can score a great massage at about half the price you'd normally pay. Thanks to student intern clinics, you can schedule an hour-long massage with a masseuse in training for $35. Student massages are available Mon through Sat. The school strictly adheres to all Texas Department of State Health Services rules and regulations. A second location is at 17043 El Camino Real (281-488-3903).

Village Massage
2635 Greenbriar Dr.
(713) 208-8840
http://villagemassage.net

If you don't like the idea of getting a massage from an intern, here's an alternative: Get one at the Village Massage, a well-known wellness center offering a full range of services. And if you're a new client, you can get a ninety-minute massage for $80 (compared to $120 regularly). New clients also receive 10 percent off other types of massages, spa treatments, and products. Package and frequent client discounts are also available.

SHAVE & A **HAIRCUT**

Aveda Institute
19241 David Memorial Dr., Shenandoah
(936) 539-6770
www.avedainstitutesbb.com

Probably the best-known place to get a student haircut, the Aveda Institute remains a great choice for anyone looking to get a fantastic cut on a budget. Open from 9:15 a.m. to 10 p.m. Tues through Fri and 9 a.m. to 3:30 on Sat, the institute gives you plenty of time to head in for a service. Prices are $15 for a cut and style, $23 for an updo, $25 for hair color, $12 for a thirty-minute manicure, and $30 for a bikini wax. A sixty-minute massage is $40; body treatments, makeup application, and facials are also available. Check the website for details.

Champion Beauty College
4714 FM 1960 Rd. West, Suite 104
(281) 583-9117
www.championbeautycollege.com

With a full range of services, from massages to pedicures to haircuts, the students at this beauty college can easily give you a head-to-toe makeover. Service prices include $6 haircuts, $25 highlights, $20 facials, $15 makeup applications, $6 manicures, and more.

CutLoose Salon
1711 Westheimer Rd.
(713) 520-7401
www.cutloosetx.com

Always wanted to be a model? A hair model, that is. Here's your chance. Cut-Loose Salon, a hip, trendy salon located in the heart of Houston, is always looking for hair models willing to allow a stylist to try out a new look. Let them do it and you score your hot new cut—free. Call for more details. The salon also gives you the option to choose a junior stylist instead of a master stylist, which will typically save you at least $10.

Mai-Trix Beauty School
13159 Northwest Freeway
(713) 957-0050
www.maitrixbeautycollege.com

This nationally accredited and fully licensed beauty school trains potential cosmetologists and hair stylists in their craft. The payoff for people who visit for a service? Massive deals. From $6 haircuts to $10 long-hair blowouts to $20 updos to $30 highlights, if you want it done, you can find it here. The school also offers facials, waxing, and body wraps.

Paul Mitchell The School
10516 Old Katy Rd., Suite A
(713) 465-6300
www.paulmitchelltheschool.com

OK, you're trusting a cosmetology student (and his or her teacher) with your head, but if you've got a little trust, it's tough to beat the price of a cut here, which is $10 for a "Phase 1" stylist and $15 for a "Phase 2" stylist. Just be ready for it to take a little longer than the average cut, since all cuts must be approved by the instructors before you're allowed to leave. Other sample weekly specials include buy-one get-one-free haircuts, free haircuts with color service, and a free blow-dry with wash. Check the online calendar for details.

V's Barbershop
2040 W. Gray St.
(713) 527-4442
www.vbarbershop.com

This is an old-school barbershop in every sense of the word, from the razor shaves, to the professional shoe shines, to the traditional haircuts with hot towels and shoulder massages. Oh, and there's also a TV at every station. Sound like a dream? Here's the best part: It's cheap, too, at less than $20 for most services. And guys, if you come with your dad or your son, they'll knock an extra $1 off each haircut.

Venus Hair
361 W. 19th St.
(713) 868-4725
www.venushairhouston.com

One of the most fun and interesting salons in Houston is hiding a giant secret: It's actually affordable. That's right, Venus Hair, located in the heart of the Heights, doesn't overcharge for its services, from great cuts to incredible Amy Winehouse beehives. Men's cuts start at $18, women's cuts start at $30, and kids' cuts start at $10. Need some color? That starts at $45.

KISS & MAKEUP

It can be hard to get good, high-quality products when you're trying to stay on a budget. But if you need to look great for a special night out, there are ways to make it happen without spending a fortune. Here are some places where you can go to get a free makeover, free beauty products, and some good advice to boot. (Yes, most of them are chains—on this topic, there's just no getting around it.)

Daily Candy
www.dailycandy.com

It's not exactly local (although hopefully they'll start doing a Houston-based arm of it soon), but Daily Candy is one of the best websites with great deals for savvy shoppers. Chock-full of interesting tidbits about new products, last-minute deals, and free giveaways, it's just the thing for any smart shopper. Just sign up online at www.dailycandy.com and you'll be the first to know what's happening where. Could it be any sweeter? I think not.

The Galleria
5085 Westheimer Rd.
(713) 622-0663
www.galleriahouston.com

In Houston we're fortunate to have this behemoth shopping Mecca at our fingertips every day of the week. But with so many stores packed into a relatively small space, it's easy to feel overwhelmed when you visit. Should you look for shoes? Purses? A new perfume? Let's simplify matters by focusing on makeup. Instead of brushing off the makeup counter ladies selling $60 foundation you'll never buy inside Neiman's or Nordstrom, stop and chat with them. Chances are good you'll learn some interesting tips, and chances are even better that they've got some free samples they can toss your way. At least it doesn't hurt to try. And if you keep on top of the various makeup websites, such as Laura Mercier or Lancôme, you can also find out about free makeover days or giveaways well before the general public.

Sephora
Multiple Houston stores
(877) 737-4672
www.sephora.com

This makeup superstore seems to have a philosophy we bargain hunters can subscribe to: If you give them samples, they will come. You get samples for buying stuff, samples for your birthday, heck, samples sometimes just for showing up in the store. More than that, nearly every product in their sprawling cosmetic wonderland has a tester attached to it, meaning you can walk in, try on whatever you want, and walk out without spending a buck. The friendly employees will even help you find the right colors for your skin tone. Score!

Wal-Mart
Multiple Houston stores
(800) 925-6278
www.walmart.com

We all have our issues with Wal-Mart, but here's one place where the giant chain got it right. On its website, Wal-Mart has a place where you can sign up for free samples of everything from detergent to toilet paper to Pop-Tarts. Frequently, the samples offered are makeup or body-care products such as foundation, body wash, whitening strips, lip gloss, and more. All you have to do is sign up on the free sample page online and check back to request free samples of your favorite makeup or beauty products. It's that easy.

CHILD'S PLAY:
CHEAP ACTIVITIES

"Children are like wet cement. Whatever falls on them makes an impression."

—DR. HAIM GINOTT

Those of you who are moms and dads probably already know the key to successful parenting: Wear the kids out during the day so they'll sleep well at night. Thankfully, in Houston there are all sorts of camps, classes, and venues for the kiddos. Whether you're looking for something athletic, studious, or just plain fun, you've got your choice in this town.

SPORTS & EXERCISE

Cypress Academy of Gymnastics and Performing Arts
11707 Huffmeister Rd.
(281) 469-4599
www.cypressacademy.com

This gymnastics academy offers everything from mommy-and-me classes up to elite programs, all designed to encourage both athleticism and confidence. Monthly tuition here is $70. Can't commit to that? The academy also hosts a variety of special events including parents' day out. Pay $15 and your child gets four hours doing gymnastics (supervised, of course) and playing in the gym. Parents' night out, birthday parties, and private lessons are also available.

Discovery Green
1500 McKinney St.
(713) 400-7336
www.discoverygreen.com

This urban park is known for its incredible event calendar, so it's only natural that some of these events would involve little ones. Every Thurs, faculty members from the Theatre Under the Stars program offer a family yoga class from 10 to 11 a.m. in the Sarofim Family Area. The classes include yoga postures, breath work, mediation, flexibility, and strength, as well as music and stories. All ages are welcome.

Fun Fair Positive Soccer
Multiple Houston locations
(800) 828-7525
www.ffps.org

The concept here is a unique one: a youth soccer league dedicated to encouraging positivity both on and off the field through special rules, training, and coaching. Taking the focus off of competition, this league accommodates a greater number of children, including nearly a hundred kids with special needs. Registration, which includes a full uniform, facilities, and trophy for every player, costs around $80 a season. The league is open to children ages four through eighteen.

Houston Gymnastics Academy
5804 S. Rice Ave.
(713) 668-6001
www.houstongymnastics.com

Is your tiny tot a rolly polly, firefly, or tumblebug? These are just some of the names of the cute classes offered at the Houston Gymnastics Academy, a local gym that teaches everything from mommy-and-me classes to cheerleading, tumbling, and trampoline classes for older kids. The gym also hosts birthday parties, parents' nights out, open gym times, and day camps. Classes start around $240 for sixteen weeks, which, if you break it down, is cheaper than a day at the movies. Class prices go up from there, depending on age.

Houston Parks and Recreation Department
Various locations around Houston
(832) 395-7012
www.houstontx.gov/parks/youthsports.html

The Houston Parks and Recreation Department offers free recreational sports programs to children ages four through eighteen living in the Houston area. Everything, from equipment to uniforms to facility usage and coaching, is completely free. Sports offered include aquatics, baseball, softball, flag football, golf, skateboarding, soccer, tennis, track and field, volleyball, and more. Call to sign up, or visit the website for more details.

K2 Academy of Kids Sports
12603 Louetta Rd., Suite 114
(281) 655-7272
www.k2academy.com

This sports academy has a little bit of everything, including cheerleading, tumbling, open play, after school care, moms' day out, holiday camps, and more. The emphasis here is making learning fun. And keeping it affordable: Classes are $60, but open play is available three times a week for just $5 a session. There's also a very reasonable mom's day out program, an adaptive gymnastics program for children with disabilities, a parents' night out program, after-school care, and more. If you register two or more children, discounts are available.

The Little Gym
14090-B Memorial Dr.
(281) 558-9500
www.thelittlegym.com

This national chain offers everything from parent-child classes for infants to cheerleading, karate, dance, and gymnastics for preschool and elementary

Mother Knows Best
The Motherhood Center
3701 W. Alabama, Suite 230
(713) 963-8880
www.motherhoodcenter.com

Before you get overwhelmed by all of the information that bombards you the minute you click on the Motherhood Center website, let's take a minute to discuss exactly what the Motherhood Center is. An all-in-one resource for both pregnant and new moms, this cool center offers services ranging from fitness and parenting classes to doula services to breast pump rentals, children's classes, and a photography studio. Basically, if it has to do with pregnancy or babies and you've ever wondered about it, they can answer your questions here. They also offer free on-site babysitting if you come in to take a class, and nanny placement services if you need a little more help at home.

school kids. The programs here are twenty weeks, so kids have a lot of time to acclimate to their teachers and surroundings. And if you pay in full, it usually works out to under $20 a session. Not sure if you want to commit? Go online and sign up for a free class. Even if it doesn't work out, it'll be a fun way for your little one to spend an afternoon without spending a cent. Check the website for information on their Houston-area locations.

StrollerFit Houston
Multiple Houston classes and locations
(888) 990-2229
www.strollerfit.com

If you're a new mom, finding time to work out can be tough. Thanks to StrollerFit, you can work out and spend time with your baby in this fifty-minute Pilates-style class created to tone mommy muscles with baby in tow. It may not sound like you'd get a very good workout this way, but having taken the classes, I can vouch that it works. Classes are open to moms with babies six weeks old and up; the first class is free. Unlimited monthly passes are $55; monthly Saturday passes for working moms are $25.

Team Tooke Mixed Martial Arts
18730 Hwy. 249
(281) 955-7300
www.teamtooke.com

Do your little ones show interest in martial arts but you're not sure they'll actually stick with it? Then the program at Team Tooke Mixed Martial Arts could be for you, because here you can get a thirty-day free trial for all classes. Kids' offerings include Little Warriors (an introduction to martial arts for ages four through six that encourages discipline and confidence), Kids Grappling (a more sophisticated look at martial arts for ages seven through thirteen), and Kids Judo (ages seven through thirteen). The free trial comes with no obligation.

THE **ARTS**

Drama Kids International
7103 Glen Chase Court
(281) 855-2555
www.dramakids.com

This acting group claims the "difference is dramatic!" at their kids' acting classes, which are offered for children starting at age four. The classes aim to enhance children's speaking and social skills and create learning abilities while also building confidence. As children get older, the classes become more technical, focusing on areas such as dramatic movement, improvisation, and scene starters, ending with a short, scripted performance for family and friends. These programs cost about $60 a month, but discounts are available. Check the website for details. Additional locations are at 14056 Southwest Freeway, Sugar Land (832-885-4869); 7040D FM 1960, Humble (281-358-6100); 6201 S. Fawnlake Dr., Katy (281-829-2287).

Fundamentally Music
5110 Spruce St.
(713) 661-1254
www.themusicclass.com

A national chain, this organization offers music classes to children as young as four months old and going up to age seven. Classes are intended to introduce music to youngsters using song, dance, singing, simple instruments, and other techniques. All children are given a CD and songbook to enjoy at home. Granted, your child isn't going to come out of class playing Mozart or acting as the lead singer of a local rock band (at least, I seriously doubt it). But the classes are good fun for kiddos and a good way of socializing them with other kids while getting them used to listening to music. Oh, and if you just want to try it out, the first lesson is free. Classes are offered at both locations (the second location is at 3455 Kirby Dr.) throughout the week; check the website for schedules and pricing.

Glazed Over Ceramic Studio
14627 Memorial Dr.
(281) 497-7272
www.glazedoverceramics.com

What's better than a few hours of creative fun? Walking out with something great to take home. At Glazed Over, kids can choose from a variety of paint-able objects, such as mugs, platters, and boxes, and decorate them with their own designs. Not into ceramics? Glass fusing and canvas painting classes are also offered. The studio also offers more regimented classes for kids ages five and up. It's open from noon to 7 p.m. on Sun, 10 a.m. to 7 p.m. on Mon, 10 a.m. to 7 p.m. on Wed, 10 a.m. to 7 p.m. on Thurs, 10 a.m. to 9 p.m. on Fri, and 10 a.m. to 9 p.m. on Sat; closed on Tues. Studio time is typically around $5, which you pay in addition to the cost of your piece. Look online for a discount coupon.

Young at Art
244 W. 19th St.
(713) 862-0900
www.youngatartstudio.net

Offerings at this studio range from paint-your-own pottery to glass fusing, wearable art, clay prints, and signature plates, as well as parties, school groups, and a ladies' night on the 19th of every month. The studio is open from 10 a.m. to 6 p.m. Wed through Sat and noon to 5 p.m. on Sun; closed Mon and Tues.

PLACES **TO** GO, **PEOPLE** TO **SEE**

Fun spots to take the kids, for free or cheap.

WEEKLY EVENTS

Alamo Drafthouse
1000 West Oaks Mall
(281) 920-9268
www.drafthouse.com/westoaks

The name may not sound particularly kid friendly (after all, they serve draft beer here to enjoy with your movies), but on Tuesday this venue, normally for children ages six and up, opens its doors to babies and toddlers for "Baby Day." During the first matinee of any show, moms and dads are welcome to bring the babes, no questions asked. So, if the last movie you saw in the theater was *Borat,* here's your chance for an update.

Children's Museum of Houston
1500 Binz St.
(713) 522-1138
www.cmhouston.org

With the city made exclusively for kids, the awesome science experiments, the art stations, and all the special events, you can't go wrong bringing kids here. But every Thursday, the experience gets even better with free admission from 5 to 8 p.m. during Free Family Night.

Dairy Ashford Roller Rink
1820 S. Dairy Ashford St.
(281) 493-5651
www.skatedarr.com

Roller-skating rinks may seem like a thing of the '80s, but on Friday at Dairy Ashford Roller Rink, they're very, very cool. That's because from 10 a.m. to noon, the rink opens itself for mommy-and-me Toddler Skate. Designed for children seven and younger, the Toddler Skate gives children (and their parents) an opportunity to skate (or scoot) around the rink. Strollers, scooters, and push toys are welcome; no bicycles are allowed. Admission is $5.

Kicks Indoor Soccer
611 Shepherd Dr.
(713) 426-1107
www.kicksindoor.com

Regularly a hub for indoor soccer, dodgeball, kickball, and even air hockey, this indoor field lets its turf field go to the tots every Friday afternoon. Open play is offered from 4 to 5:30 p.m.; parents must supervise their children during this time. Admission is $5 per child.

SEMI-REGULAR EVENTS

AMC Movie Theaters
Multiple Houston locations
www.amcentertainment.com

It's getting more and more difficult to find a good deal at the movie theater, which is why I appreciate AMC's offering discount showtimes. Every Mon through Thurs, all shows are half price, as are shows screening before noon Fri through Sun. The theaters also sometimes host special "autism sensory friendly shows" designed to cater to children with special needs, particularly autism.

Harris County Public Library
Held at numerous library locations
(713) 749-9000
www.hcpl.net

This public library system offers multiple events on a daily basis for children, from *Cat In the Hat*–themed story times to pajama times to arts and crafts; there's always something to do—for free—with the kids. Check the website for details and branch locations.

Houston Area Live Steamers
Zube Park
17802 Roberts Rd., Hockley
www.hals.org

You might not have heard of the Houston Area Live Steamers before, but if you've got a little one who's into trains, you're going to want to listen up. This interesting group creates steam model trains that are big enough to ride. Starting around 9 a.m. on the third Sat of every month, the group shows up in Zube Park and offers free train rides (typically until 3 p.m.) to the general public. Try to get there early to avoid waiting in line.

Houston Public Library
Held at numerous library locations
(see Appendix D for a full list of libraries)
(832) 393-1313
www.hpl.lib.tx.us

From bilingual story times to fire truck visits, the Houston Public Library hosts a variety of free events throughout the week that are great for children of all ages. A sample of events offered at the various branches includes baby time, toddler time, Chinese story time, bedtime story time, children's story time, and craft time. Check the website for a full calendar of events; register in advance.

Main Street Theater
2540 Times Blvd.
(713) 524-6706
www.mainstreettheater.com

Been craving a date night with your sweetie? No problem. At the Main Street Theater, you can enjoy a first-rate show while the kids play games right next door as part of the Parent Play Date option. Open to children ages six through eleven and run by staff of the theater's Kids On Stage program, Parent Play Date is offered certain Saturdays during each run. The cost is $20 for the first child and $15 for any additional children, plus the cost of your theater tickets. Call or check the website to register in advance.

Do Unto Others: Volunteering

Music classes, bouncy castles, and train rides are great, but if you really want to get your kids off to a good start, why not volunteer with them? There are lots of organizations in Houston that would love to have help from every member of your family. Here are some helpful links to organizations that help place or are looking for volunteers.

Volunteer Houston: www.volunteerhouston.org
Volunteer Match: www.volunteermatch.org
Harris County Citizen Corps: www.harriscountycitizencorps.com
Make-A-Wish Foundation: www.wish.org
Houston SPCA: www.spcahouston.org
Volunteer Initiatives Program: www.houstontx.gov/volunteer

ALWAYS **FUN**

Barnes & Noble
Multiple Houston locations
(713) 629-8828
www.barnesandnoble.com

These popular stores offer a little bit of everything, and children's events are no exception. Most stores offer weekly story times; some offer events for children more often than that. Expect upbeat readers, a small crowd, and a good time for kids of all ages. Call ahead to confirm details. Regular readings, writers' groups, and book clubs are also available here.

Blue Bell Creamery
1101 S. Blue Bell Rd., Brenham
(800) 327-8135
www.bluebell.com

It's hard to go wrong when you take kids to a creamery, especially when it's as fun and delicious as the offerings at Blue Bell. After you watch a video about the history of the company, you'll get to tour the winding halls, seeing break rooms where workers "eat all we can and sell the rest" and watching as batches of ice cream are poured into awaiting half-gallon cartons. At the end you'll be treated to a free helping of ice cream—any flavor you like. Tours are offered at 10 and 11 a.m. and 1, 1:30, 2, and 2:30 p.m.; no weekend tours are available. Tours are $5 for adults, $3 for seniors fifty-five and over and children six through fourteen, and free for school groups and children under six.

Hermann Park
6001 Fannin St.
(713) 845-1000
www.hermannpark.org

For a day outside, you can't beat Hermann Park, which is filled with outdoor activities perfect for children of all ages. Start at the railroad, which runs through the park from 10 a.m. to 5:30 p.m. Mon through Fri and 10 a.m. to 6 p.m. Sat through Sun. Tickets are $3 per person; children under eleven months are free. Buy tickets in the Hermann Park Conservancy Gift Shop, located at Kinder Station adjacent to the Houston Zoo main entrance. Then head over for some pedal boating, which is $9 for a thirty-minute ride. The boats are available from 11 a.m. to 5 p.m. daily. One rider in each boat must be eighteen with valid ID.

Jumpin' Jak's
3403 FM 1960
(281) 537-8833
www.jumpinjaks.net

Do your kids love to make believe? Then take them to Jumpin' Jak's, a children's play area filled with miniature structures, climbing walls, bridges, and more. Think of it as a giant tree house. Jumpin' Jak's is open from 9 a.m. to 9 p.m. Mon through Fri. Admission is "pay your age," with a $5 maximum limit.

Monkey Bizness
750 W. Sam Houston Parkway North, Suite 170
(832) 237-0100
www.monkeybizness.com

If your kids like to bounce, then you can't pass up this open-play, bouncy-castle wonderland. Filled with amenities such as slides, castles, and rock-climbing walls, Monkey Bizness is a dream come true for little ones. And every weekday between 10 a.m. and 6 p.m., the staff hosts open playtime, when all ages can play freely. Admission is $7.50 each for children ages one through eighteen (children under age one are free with a paying sibling). If you arrive before 11 a.m. Mon, Thurs, and Fri, admission is only $5.

The Orange Show Monument
2402 Munger St.
(713) 926-6368
www.orangeshow.org

This fantastic art space claims to celebrate "the artist in everyone," and that includes kids. Created out of folk art (and sometimes junk), this cool museum/art space/playground was created by Jefferson Davis McKissack between 1956 and 1979. Featuring areas such as a stage, a pond, a wishing well, a gift shop, and several upper platforms, this is a great place to go and get lost. Interesting accessories, such as mannequins, tractor seats, and wagon wheels surprise around every corner. Special events take place throughout the year. The museum is open from noon to 5 p.m. on Sat and Sun; admission is $1.

Playhouse 1960
6814 Gant Rd., Suite 116
(281) 587-8243
www.ph1960.com

This nonprofit community theater has been around since 1973, offering a variety of shows such as *Murder on the Nile, Bye Bye Birdie,* and *White Christmas.* For youngsters, however, the real draw is the Young Actor's Theater, which offers performances of shows such as *Alice in Wonderland Jr., Aladdin Jr.,* and *The Wizard of Oz.* Youth stage tickets are $8. Check the website for upcoming shows.

The Showboat Drive-In
22422 FM 2920 Rd., Hockley
(281) 351-5224
www.theshowboatdrivein.com

Located about forty minutes away in Hockley, this authentic drive-in theater harkens back to the days of sock hops and poodle skirts. Double features are shown Fri, Sat, and Sun; gates open at 7 p.m. Movies start at dusk, and a full concession stand is available. Most movies are new releases. Admission is $5 for adults, $4 for children three through twelve, and free for babies. Cash only.

Studio Movie Grill
805 Town and Country Lane
(713) 461-4449
www.studiomoviegrill.com

It may be known for its delicious food and drinks, but if you're looking for somewhere to go with the kids, this would be it—thanks to some seriously kid-friendly options such as Kidtoons, which are offered every weekend at 11 a.m. Admission is just $2. Have a child with special needs? Studio Movie Grill also offers certain "special needs" screenings with free admission, as well as softer sound and brighter lighting. Check the website for details. A second location is in Copperfield at 8580 Hwy. 6 North (832-593-6684).

KIDS' MENU

Going out to eat as a family can be an expensive venture, and we all know that not all restaurants are kid friendly. But it is entirely possible to go to a place that will welcome you and your whole brood without charging an arm and a leg—in fact, some places even offer free meals for the kiddos.

Boudreaux's Cajun Kitchen
12806 Gulf Freeway
(281) 464-6800
www.boudreauxs.net

This place is known locally for its delicious Cajun options, but on Tuesday it's even more well known for its kids-eat-free special. Just buy one adult entree for $6.95 or more and get a kid's meal free. Other specials are also available throughout the week. Check out their website for information on their four other Houston locations.

Brian O'Neill's Irish Pub
5555 Morningside Dr.
(713) 522-2603
www.brianoneills.com

A pub may not seem like the most kid friendly spot for lunch, but if you go on a Saturday kids eat free with the purchase of one regular-priced entree. The deal is available from 11 a.m. to 6 p.m. and open to kids twelve and under. Kids' fare includes a mini cheeseburger, chicken tenders, grilled cheese, hot dog, pizza, mac and cheese, and shepherd's pie.

Candelari's Pizzeria
6002 Washington Ave.
(832) 200-1474
www.candelaris.com

If you're looking for great pizza, you won't go wrong here, with toppings ranging from ground turkey to gorgonzola to roasted grape tomatoes. If you go with the kiddos, try to go Mon through Wed, when kids receive an item from the kids' menu free with the purchase of any regularly priced adult entree or pizza. The offer is for dining in only. Check the website for information on Candelari's four other Houston-area locations.

El Palenque Mexican Restaurant and Cantina
10803 Westheimer Rd.
(713) 706-4485
www.gopalenque.com

This joint is cool for several reasons. First, the authentic Tex-Mex and margaritas here are really, really good. Plus, the atmosphere is fun and boisterous, perfect for little ones hoping to be entertained. And finally, it's great because it has free ice cream, since any place with free ice cream rules. Additional locations are in Houston at 21161 Tomball Parkway (281-376-6960) and in Spring at 1485 Spring Cypress Rd. (281-353-4055).

Ikea Houston
7810 Katy Freeway
(713) 688-7867
www.ikea.com

Shopping til you drop? Take a break in the Ikea restaurant, where kids' meals, featuring items such as pasta, meatballs, mac and cheese, and peanut butter and jelly sandwiches, are just 99 cents each. Pick three for $2.49.

Lupe Tortilla Mexican Restaurant
Multiple Houston-area locations
www.lupetortilla.com

One word describes the magnetic draw of this place to parents: playground. Many of these local locations have an ample playground perfect for entertaining the youngsters while you sip on a margarita. Just make sure you keep an eye on the little ones—lots of parents here don't. Location not have a playground? It's still worth a trip for the melt-in-your-mouth quesadillas, sizzling fajitas, and enormous salads.

Red Onion Mexican Grill
13147 Northwest Freeway
(713) 690-1403
www.caferedonion.com

This Mexican grill impresses families with free kids' meals for children ten and under every Wed through Fri. Oh, and parents, you won't mind the delicious selection of drinks or tasty dishes, either.

ADULT EDUCATION:
DO IT WITH CLASS

*"Why don't they pass a constitutional amend-
ment prohibiting anybody from learning anything? If it works as well as Prohibition did, in
five years Americans would be the smartest race
of people on Earth."*

—WILL ROGERS

If you think school is just for tykes, think again. If there's something you've always wanted to learn, Houston's got your back, from dancing to cooking to sketching scantily clad models. Even better news? Many of the classes are free or offered for a nominal fee. There are also informal classes offered at some of the universities that may be worth checking into. Just make sure you register for most beforehand, as schedules, dates, and times may change.

DIRTY **DANCING**

Get rid of those two left feet on the cheap!

Big Texas Dance Hall and Saloon
19959 Holzwarth Rd., Spring
(281) 353-8898
www.bigtexassaloon.com/spring.html

Feeling a little too intimidated to take a swing around the dance floor? Just arrive early at Big Texas and receive free dance lessons from 7 to 8 p.m. every Wed. You'll be looking like a pro in no time. Admission is free, and happy hour specials include $1.75 wells, $1.75 calls, $1.75 longnecks, and $1.75 house wine.

Bluebonnet Squares Square Dancing
Events are at the Spring Woods
United Methodist Church
1711 FM 1960 West
www.bluebonnets.irisar.com

Think square dancing is for squares? Think again. This upbeat square-dancing group knows how to have a good time, hosting weekly events for enthusiasts of the dance. Interested in learning? They also host regular beginner nights and lessons. Check the website for details.

Dance Factory Houston
17619 FM 529
(281) 859-9383
www.dancefactoryhouston.com

This dance venue frequently hosts special events and socials on weekends for $5. Call for details. Classes are also offered here in areas such as hip-hop, ballet, jazz, and tap dancing.

Downtown Aquarium
410 Bagby St.
(713) 223-3474
www.aquariumrestaurants.com

One of the most popular attractions in Houston also hosts a flourishing free salsa night on Friday throughout the summer. Held from 7 to 11 p.m., the "Latin Beats" event includes free salsa dance lessons from seasoned professionals and delicious food and drinks at a discounted price. Check the website for schedule.

Elvia's Cantina
2727 Fondren Rd.
(713) 266-9631

An alternative to the glitzy scene at Sullivan's is Elvia's, which has been well known among Houston's elite salsa dancing community for years now. On Wednesday nights in particular the band is kickin' and the place is packed with people who seem to have been dancing the salsa since the time they could walk. The crowd is friendly and international, and don't worry if someone asks you to dance in a language other than you own. After all, body language is all you really need on the dance floor.

➤Hope Stone Ballet
1210 W. Clay St.
(713) 526-1907
www.hopestoneinc.org

Instead of sitting through yet another performance of *The Nutcracker* this winter, why not star in it? Hope Stone Ballet teaches the graceful dance to all levels, from beginners and children to professionals. Added bonus? Many classes are accompanied by a live piano soundtrack. Classes are about $12.50 a session, or $130 for an unlimited pass. The center also hosts free and low-fee events throughout the year; check the website for details.

Houston Swing Dance Society
Barbara King Dance Studio
5410 Bellaire Blvd., Bellaire
www.hsds.org

Do you have a brand new pair of saddle shoes you're dying to break in or a new partner to try out? Whatever it is, you want to swing dance, and you want to do it now. Then you're in luck. Every Sun from 8:30 to 10:30 p.m., the Houston Swing Dance Society hosts public dance parties for $7. A variety of classes, also held on Sun, are also available.

Omni Salsa Studio
5615 Richmond Ave.
(832) 875-2846
www.omnisalsa.com

Offering everything from salsa to tango to belly dancing, this is a nice place to try if you're not yet sure what kind of dance you're interested in. The studio offers a free class to newcomers and also offers reduced rates for group lessons starting around $10 a class. Private classes are also available.

Southwest Whip Club
Classes are held at Memorial City DanceSport Center
14520 Memorial Dr.
(281) 558-0369
www.swwc.org

No, this isn't *that* kind of whip: You're more likely to see this dance in *Happy Days* than at an S & M convention. This modern type of swing is increasingly gaining ground with the help of organizations such as the Southwest Whip Club, which dedicates every Wednesday night to practicing it. Classes last an hour, from 8 to 9 p.m., and are held weekly. The cost is $40 a month for members, or $15 a class for nonmembers.

SSQQ
4803 Bissonnet St.
(713) 861-1906
www.ssqq.com

This swing-dance Mecca has been instructing potential swingers for decades, so if you're interested in learning this popular dance, or other varieties such as salsa, whip, and ballroom dancing, this is the place to come. The instructors are smart, informative, and lots of fun, so you should be pretty confident that you'll get bang for your buck. Four two-hour classes are $50 for men, $40 for women. Private classes are also available. SSQQ also offers free practice nights after class most evenings, so you can try out your just-learned techniques. The best part? Even if you're not taking a class, you can attend the weekend dance parties for a nominal fee, typically $5 for the evening.

Sullivan's Steakhouse
4608 Westheimer Rd.
(713) 961-0333
www.sullivansteakhouse.com

Every Wednesday, the bar area of this high-end steak house fills with salsa dancers eager to find a new dance partner, new friend, or new fling. The payoff for salsa wannabes is lots of people to dance with who are really, really good. Never danced salsa before? Just as well. The crowd here is more than happy to teach you. Admission is free.

Wild West
6101 Richmond Ave.
(713) 266-2282
www.wildwesthouston.com

One of the city's favorite spots for country and western dancing, this sprawling, oak-planked dance hall is also a great place for tentative two-steppers to learn the craft. Every Sunday night, the club offers free dance lessons from 4:30 to 6 p.m., followed by a free fajita dinner. Can't make it on Sun? Try Thurs, when pool is free all night long.

WHAT'S **COOKIN'?**

Get your grub on—and impress your date—at these fun cooking schools.

Cake Craft Shoppe
3530 Hwy. 6, Sugar Land
(281) 491-3920
www.cakecraftshoppe.com

Always wanted to learn how to make one of those scrumptious icing roses? Here's your chance. Cake Craft Shoppe offers a variety of cake decorating classes that will teach you all the skills you'll need to compete with even the most experienced Cake Boss. The beginner class costs $50 (including a starter kit) for nine hours of class that will teach you about equipment, baking, preparing a cake for decoration, icing basics, writing, borders, roses, flowers, and figure piping.

Camp Cook
7058 Lakeview Haven Dr.
(281) 855-9779
www.camp-cook.org

This local organization has classes for all levels, from preschoolers up to adults. Topics vary and are affordably priced—mommy-and-me classes are $20 for two participants; date-night classes are around $75 a couple for a two-hour class that includes a three-course dinner.

Well Done Cooking Classes
1208 E. 29th St.
(832) 782-3518
www.welldonecc.com

This local cooking school specializes in making great cooking accessible to the general public. As part of this, they regularly offer on their website discounted classes and package deals (a recent deal offered up to 50 percent off a second class with the company). Class options focus on categories such as skills, baking, dinner parties, and holidays.

Williams Sonoma
4060 Westheimer Rd.
(713) 212-0346
www.williams-sonoma.com

Sure, it's a chain, but when a chain does something well, it definitely deserves a mention. Every week this upscale cooking store offers free technique classes and product demonstrations that are both informative and entertaining. Cooking classes and book signings are also available. Check the website for details and information on their four other Houston-area locations.

ARTS, **CRAFTS** & **MEDIA**

Not sure what kind of class you're looking for? Here are some other options.

Dr. Sketchy
Held every second Sunday at
Avant Garden, 411 Westheimer Rd.
http://houstonsketchy.com

Between the scantily clad models, drinks at the bar, and free snacks, there's nothing not to like about this monthly live drawing class, where "cabaret meets art school." Just show up with your art supplies, grab a seat at one of the tables, and put your pencil to the pad. Need more inspiration? Model themes in recent classes have included pinups, pirates, and bondage. But don't worry—women are welcome, too. Admission is $10, plus tips for the model.

Glazed Over Ceramic Studio
14627-B Memorial Dr.
(281) 497-7272
www.glazedoverceramics.com

Paint-your-own pottery classes have been popular for a while now, but here's a twist: This ceramics studio also offers glass fusing and canvas painting, all for a low price. It's perfect for budding artists who haven't yet found their niche, and it's BYOB so you can get a buzz while you try to figure it out. Special themed nights and parties are also available. Check the website for discount coupons.

Houston Media Source
410 Roberts St.
(713) 524-7700
http://hmstv.org

Houston Media Source is the perfect place for anyone who's ever wanted to start their own TV show but didn't know quite how to do it. Not only does Houston's public access channel offer a forum for all kinds of shows, it also offers comprehensive training courses in areas such as media literacy, shooting, lighting, and sound. The classes are inexpensive, and once you take them, you qualify to check out equipment from HMS's impressive media room. You can shoot shows on-site or off campus.

Sew Crafty
321-B 19th St.
(713) 863-1144
www.sewcraftyhouston.com

Ever wondered how to make a quilt, a pair of toe socks, or some awesome pajama pants? Here's your chance. Sew Crafty, Houston's only craft studio and sewing lounge, offers frequent classes on all kinds of crafts. Classes start around $40 and typically include all materials.

Southwest Casting
www.southwestcasting.com

Lights, camera, action! Always wanted to act but not sure how you'd fit in? Southwest Casting is a casting agency that has placed actors with shows such as *Friday Night Lights* and *Judge Alex*, in commercials with major businesses such as American Express and Luby's, and even in music videos for artists such as Pat Green and Paul Wall. Simply sign up for their mailing list and keep an eye out for when they need extras. It's just like an acting class, for free. In fact, extras often get paid.

HOLA! **BONJOUR!** JAMBO!

Stepping up your linguistic game doesn't have to be expensive. Here are some places that will help you learn a new language for only a few clams.

Bilingual Education Institute
6060 Richmond Ave., Suite 180
(713) 789-4555
www.aetas.com

This company offers both intensive and casual Spanish classes for individuals, corporations, nonprofits, and youth. Evening and Saturday classes are available for working students; discounts are available.

Gonzales School of Languages

7500 San Felipe, Suite 600
(713) 419-1035
www.gonzaleslanguages.com

In addition to teaching fundamentals of the language, the staff of native Spanish speakers at the Gonzales School of Languages also focuses on teaching about the culture of the country through personal anecdotes. Class levels range from beginner to expert. Private, semiprivate, and corporate classes are available, as is a work-from-home package that allows you to study at your own pace. Sign up for a free class online, and register for Thursday classes for an added discount. Classes also meet monthly for casual meet-ups to socialize and practice the language.

HABLA Houston Spanish School

(832) 646-3426
www.hablahouston.com

This school has made it a mission to offer affordable Spanish classes to the Houston community, and with classes offered in a variety of locations for everyone from kids to business people, chances are good you can find something to mesh with your schedule. Discounts are offered for early registration; other discounts may be available online.

EXTENDING **YOUR** EDUCATION

A city the size of Houston is bound to have some great universities, and when you're looking for a quick learning fix, there's no better place to turn. Many of the colleges and universities offer extended education classes to local residents looking to learn something new. Here are three of the best extended education programs.

Houston Community College's School of Continuing Education

Multiple Houston locations
(713) 718-2000
www.hccs.edu

Whether you want to earn a degree or just take a couple of courses, Houston Community College is a good way to test the waters on a new subject. The Continuing Education program offers nonstudents courses on topics such as advertising, nursing, writing, construction, public safety, languages, computers, and more.

Rice University's Glasscock School of Continuing Studies
6100 Main St., MS-550, at Rice University
(713) 348-4803
www.gscs.rice.edu

One of the state's most prominent universities also has a multitude of classes on subjects ranging from studio art and photography to personal finance to creative writing and foreign language classes. Basically, if you want to learn it, they probably offer it. Favorite courses include "retirement in the new economy," "introduction to digital photography," and "historic Houston neighborhoods."

University of Houston Continuing Education
102 C. N. Hilton Hotel and College
at the University of Houston
(713) 743-1060
www.uh.edu/continuingeducation

This program is tailored to professionals seeking certificates, courses, workshops, conferences, online courses, and custom-designed training in specific subject areas. Some of the courses are free, while others charge a fee. Topics range from LSAT preparation to pharmacy technology to iPhone programming. Check the website for details and costs.

OUTDOORS:
PARKS & RECREATION

"Of course I have played outdoor games. I once played dominoes in an open air cafe in Paris."

—OSCAR WILDE

Houston's overarching reputation for smog and traffic masks a little secret about the city: It's actually an extremely outdoorsy place. Sure, you may have to seek places out a little more than you might in neighboring cities such as Austin, but if you look, you will most certainly find plenty of places to breathe in the outside air, enjoy the trees, and soak in a little sun. From parks to outdoor art exhibits to random bat colonies, there's a little something outside for everyone. You just have to look.

DESTINATION **PARKS**

(For a full list of area parks, see Appendix E. For a full list of hiking and biking trails, see Appendix F.)

Bear Creek Pioneers Park
3535 War Memorial Dr.
(281) 496-2177
www.co.harris.tx.us

Soccer fans across Houston already know about this park, which is a hub for soccer games of all kinds on weekends. But even if soccer isn't your sport of choice, there are lots of other things to do within this 2,000-acre park, such as tennis, hiking, softball, baseball, horseshoes, and a playground. The many paths are also a nice place for road bikers to take a ride. The park may not be the most centrally located in Houston, but the diverse offerings here make it worth the trip.

Hermann Park
6001 Fannin St.
(713) 845-1000
www.hermannpark.org

With its pedal boats, Japanese garden, reflecting pool, fountains, and miniature train, Hermann Park is one of the greatest places to spend a day in Houston—particularly if you're traveling with kids. Its location next to the Houston Zoo, the Museum of Fine Arts, and the Museum of Natural Science doesn't hurt, either. Just make sure you pack the sunscreen—that summer sun can be brutal. Also, if you join the Hermann Park Conservancy, you'll get free train and pedal boat tickets.

MacGregor Park
Old Spanish Trail and Martin Luther King Jr. Boulevard
(713) 748-0317
www.houstontx.gov/parks

The jogging trail in this community park stretches for 12.5 miles, but if that seems a little excessive to you, other, less strenuous options include a swimming pool, picnic areas, community center, tennis center, disc golf course, and more. Wear your bug spray, though. The park's location adjacent to Brays Bayou can attract insects, particularly in summer.

 Memorial Park
6501 Memorial Dr.
(713) 863-8403
www.memorialparkconservancy.org

When you're the seventy-second largest park in the US, you'd better have quite a bit to offer your visitors. Thankfully, Memorial Park does. Known for its fantastic 3-mile running loop, this park in the center of the city is also home to tennis courts, a swimming pool, mountain-biking trails, a paved in-line skating and biking loop, bocce courts, baseball fields, a playground, and more. Many intramural leagues and fitness classes also meet here.

DOG **PARKS**

Danny Jackson Bark Park
4700 Westpark Dr., near US 610
www.co.harris.tx.us

Its location inside the loop makes this dog park popular among dog lovers. The many amenities at the park, such as separate large and small dog areas, ponds, trees, benches, and walking paths, don't hurt, either. Tip: Go early on weekends. The parks can get crowded.

Ervan Chew Dog Park

4502 Dunlavy St.
www.houstontx.gov/parks

Expect a large, fenced-in park with pickup bags, fountains, benches, and shade trees. The nearby swimming pool, playground, and picnic area will delight youngsters of the two-legged variety as well.

Maxey Park

601 Maxey Rd.
www.houstontx.gov/parks

The second official dog park established under the Houston Parks and Recreation system, Maxey Park impresses with more than a dozen acres of parkland for pets. Features include a fenced, off-leash area, doggie drinking fountains, showers, waste disposal stations, and benches.

Millie Bush Bark Park

16756 Westheimer Parkway
www.co.harris.tx.us

Multiple fire hydrants, pickup bags, swimming ponds, fountains, shade areas, showers, and benches make this bark park a doggie heaven. Restrooms and picnic benches are located near the park as well. Open daily.

T. C. Jester Park

4201 W. T. C. Jester Blvd.
(713) 686-6800
www.houstontx.gov/parks

With separate runs for big and small dogs, this recently opened dog park offers more than one acre of space for dogs to run and play. Whether they burrow in the mountains of wood chips or splash in well-placed plastic baby pools, your pooches will enjoy their time here.

Need Some Doggone Help?

Speaking of your four-legged best friend, there may be times in your life that you'll need a hand or two with your pooch. Going out of town and need a sitter for the weekend? Want somewhere Fido can play with other dogs while you're at work? Or just sick of the mess in your backyard? Here are some of the best, most affordable dog-related services in town.

Blue Moon Doga

(832) 573-2217

http://site.bluemoondoga.com

File this one under bizarre but awesome: Blue Moon Doga offers yoga classes—for dogs. One quick call and your pooch could be doing the downward dog (no pun intended) with the best of them. "Whether you want to enjoy doga with a young animal or an older animal, you need expert guidance to effectively become one with your dog," the website states. Classes are $30 for a half-hour private class and $20 for a half-hour group class, although discounts are available. Web cam classes, meaning you take the class from home using a web cam, are also available for the same price.

Bow Wow Beach Club

1618 Webster St.

(713) 658-0900

www.urbantails.cc

Life's a beach—or at least it should be. And that goes for your dog, too. If you've been looking for a change of pace from the everyday dog park, why not try the Bow Wow Beach Club, where your pup can take a dip at a dogs-only indoor pool? Free sessions with swim instructors are available for puppies six months and under on the first Thurs of every month. Life jackets and treats are included (yes, seriously). Reserve in advance. For older dogs, open swim is also available. Urban Tails also offers doggie day care (with a doggie cam, so you can watch what she's doing from your work computer) and overnight boarding, as well as other activities such as storytelling sessions, playtime in the outdoor gym, massages, and lots of cuddles and pats. Check the website for details or to arrange a facility tour.

Houston Dog Ranch
9602 Dalecrest Dr.
(713) 465-2275
www.houstondogranch.com
Heading out of town and can't take your pooch? Then leave him with Houston Dog Ranch, a doggie day-care and training facility that also offers weekend assistance. Located on a sprawling property with a dog-bone-shaped doggie swimming pool, this place is like a spa for dogs. The caregivers are friendly and warm and really seem to have the dogs' best interests in mind. When we left our puppy here over-night, they even moved her into the manager's office because they thought she would feel more comfortable there than in one of the big kennels outside. Grooming, workshops, and training classes are also available. There's even a bus that will pick up and drop off your dogs if you can't transport them to the ranch. Talk about hospitality. Overnight rates start at around $35.

Wholly Krap Dog Waste Removal
1963 Round Spring Dr., Humble
(281) 359-3647
www.whollykrap.com
You've probably been in this position a thousand times. You go out into the backyard to take out the trash, and bam—you step in a giant, er, present, from man's best friend. You've been meaning to shovel the yard, but between work, the kids, and a recent vacation, you just haven't had time. Well, Wholly Krap—here's your solution. Wholly Krap is a dog-waste removal service that comes to your house (whether you're home or not) and cleans up. Yes, such services exist, and they are worth every cent. Prices start at $13 a week for one dog, but multiple discounts are available on the website. Call for information and quotes.

GET **OUT**

Even though Houston isn't really known for its green spaces, there are plenty of unique, beautiful places where you can get some fresh air. Seeking something a little different? Here are some non-park options that are sure to entertain.

• Cactus King
625 W. Canino Rd., off I-45
(281) 591-8833
www.thecactusking.com

It may not be an attraction in the most traditional sense of the word, but Cactus King is definitely a must see for anyone living in or visiting Houston. Owner Lyn Rathburn offers more than 250 species of cactus as well as other succulents. It's free to visit, but if you want to take home a souvenir, you can find plants for as low as $1. And don't miss Rathburn's incredible handmade folk art.

• Houston Arboretum and Nature Center
4501 Woodway Dr.
(713) 681-8433
www.houstonarboretum.org

With roughly 155 acres of trails and trees, this nonprofit nature sanctuary adjacent to Memorial Park is the perfect place to escape for a while. The nature trails, which are free to hike and total a distance of 5 miles, make it easy to get some exercise and get an education on native plants and animals. Want to get more involved? The arboretum also offers a variety of classes, for a fee.

• Houston Japanese Garden
6001 Fannin, in Hermann Park
(713) 524-5876
www.hermannpark.org

The definition of serene, the Japanese Garden in Hermann Park is the perfect place to chill out on a sunny afternoon. Its stone paths, waterfalls, bridges, sculptures, and abundant wildlife make for a nice stroll, and its wide benches and well-placed pagodas give you plenty of places to rest. Nature lovers will love this green-filled park.

Jesse H. Jones Park & Nature Center
20634 Kenswick Dr., Humble
(281) 446-8588
www.hcp4.net/jones

The park's location next to Spring Creek gives it a diverse and rich natural spectrum that includes swampland, white-sand beaches, and forest climates. Activities and points of interest offered within the park include biking and hiking trails, bird and bat boxes, wildlife feeders, a nature center, pavilions, barbecue grills, and more.

Lee and Joe Jamail Skatepark
103 Sabine St.
(713) 222-5500
www.houstonparksboard.org

If you're into grinding, kick flipping, and ollieing, you don't want to miss this amazing, 30,000-square-foot skate park, which opened in 2008 and was intended to give skateboard and in-line skating enthusiasts a place near downtown to practice their craft. Not into skating? Stop by to see the urban art display, the brainchild of the Houston Parks Board and the Orange Show Center for Visionary Art.

• Lillie and Hugh Roy Cullen Sculpture Garden
Next to the Museum of Fine Arts at the
corner of Montrose Boulevard and Bissonnet Street
(713) 639-7300
www.mfah.org/sculpturegarden

Don't want to pay the entry fee for the Museum of Fine Arts? No problem! Just head next door, where you'll find this lovely outdoor sculpture garden, which opened in 1986 and is filled with more than twenty-five sculptures by artists such as Henri Matisse, Frank Stella, and Louise Bourgeois. Serene and shaded, this is a perfect spot for quiet reflection or an educational date.

**San Jacinto Battleground State Historical Park
and Battleship *Texas***
Off Highway 225 East, about 20 miles from downtown
(281) 479-2421
www.sanjacinto-museum.org
If you're a history buff—or interested in Texas history at all—you'll
enjoy a visit to this park, which is home to the San Jacinto Museum
(which offers history and artifacts from Mexican Texas, the Texas Rev-
olution, and the Republic of Texas), the San Jacinto Memorial Monument (the world's tallest monument tower), and Battleship *Texas* (the
first battleship memorial museum in the US). Admission to the park
is only $1, although the museum and battleship charge additional
entrance fees.

Mercer Arboretum & Botanic Gardens
22306 Aldine Westfield Rd., Humble
(281) 443-8731
www.hcp4.net/mercer

This lovely garden, located just outside the city, is a nice change of pace
from the regular Houston haunts. Located in the East Texas Piney Woods,
this 300-acre facility offers activities such as bird watching, canoeing and
kayaking, plant and animal identification, fishing, and hiking, as well as
picnic areas, a playground, and a teahouse.

Sea Center Texas
300 Medical Dr., Lake Jackson
(979) 292-0100
www.tpwd.state.tx.us

Want Sea World without the crazy admission costs? Try Sea Center Texas, a
fantastic little nature center, aquarium, and fish hatchery that is always free
to the public. Little ones in particular will love this facility, which offers an
up-close view of creatures such as sharks, eels, and snapper. Hike through

the on-site wetland, learn about breeding in the hatchery, or get your hands dirty in the well-stocked touch tank. It's about forty-five minutes outside of Houston, but worth the drive.

Waugh Bridge Bat Colony
Waugh Drive Bridge over Buffalo Bayou,
between Allen Parkway and Memorial Drive
(713) 752-0314
www.buffalobayou.org/WaughBatColony.htm

An estimated 300,000 Mexican free-tailed bats are said to call this bridge, located just a stone's throw from downtown, home. Each night around dusk, the bats emerge to find food, exiting the bridge in an impressive black cloud. The best time to see the bats is Mar through Sept. If you want a firsthand view of the bats from the water, call the Buffalo Bayou Partnership to reserve a spot on the Bat Colony Pontoon Boat Tour.

Williams Tower and Waterwall
2800 Post Oak Blvd.
(713) 850-8841

The tallest building in Houston outside of downtown is the Williams Tower, which stands at an impressive 909 feet. In its shadow is the Williams Waterwall, a gushing fountain complex designed by Philip Johnson. Make sure you bring the kids—and bring bread to feed the ducks that live near the Waterwall. This is the perfect place for a picnic.

INSIDE SCOOP: CHEAP OUTDOOR DEALS

From the space center to the zoo to the aquarium, Houston is known for its destination attractions. The only problem? The admission costs are frequently much higher than most people want to pay. But with a little research, you can score excellent discounts at these places.

Downtown Aquarium
401 Bagby St.
(713) 223-3474
www.aquariumrestaurants.com

General admission here is a relatively affordable $10, but if you plan to spend the day here and experience all of the different amusements (the aquarium also has a variety of rides and games), you'll want to get a $15.99 all-day adventure pass, which offers access to exhibits and unlimited rides. Don't miss the amazing tunnel of sharks, the majestic white tigers, or the fascinating, hands-on Discovery Rig. The website also frequently offers two-for-one deals. Check regularly for updates.

Houston Zoo
1513 Cambridge St.
(713) 533-6500
www.houstonzoo.org

Getting in to the see the apes at this Houston hot spot will cost you more than a bushel of bananas, but if you're smart about your timing, you can save a bundle—or even go for free. The zoo offers free admission on the first Tues of the month from 2 p.m. to closing time. Want to go more often? Consider becoming a member. The $55 individual membership goes to a good cause and gets you and a guest free visits for a year.

Houston CityPass
If you're planning to visit multiple attractions, consider buying the Houston CityPass, which costs $39 and gets you access to six of Houston's best attractions. Just flash your pass and skip the lines. The CityPass gets you admission to Space Center Houston, the Downtown Aquarium, the Houston Zoo, and the Houston Museum of Natural Science, as well as your choice of the Museum of Fine Arts or the Children's Museum of Houston and George Ranch Historical Park or The Health Museum.

Kemah Boardwalk
215 Kipp Ave., Kemah
(281) 334-9880
www.kemahboardwalk.com

This Landry's-owned entertainment complex features rides, games, restaurants, and even a hotel sure to please visitors of all ages. For a deal, check the website, where you can find specials ranging from discounted all-day ride passes to coupons for $1.99 kids' meals.

Space Center Houston
1601 NASA Parkway
(281) 244-2100
www.spacecenter.org

Becoming a member is the best way to go at this popular attraction. An annual individual membership is $22.95 (for perspective, regular one-time admission is $19.95) and grants you free admission for a year. If you don't want to become a member, try booking your tickets online. You can usually receive $5 off or more by doing so.

HEALTH & MEDICAL:
AN APPLE A DAY

"My doctor gave me six months to live, but when I couldn't pay the bill, he gave me six months more."

—WALTER MATTHAU

Here's one great thing about living in Houston: our medical community. From our cancer researchers to our children's hospitals, it's top notch. So if you're looking for free or inexpensive medical care, chances are good you'll have an easier time finding it here than you might elsewhere.

Here's a breakdown of some of the best places to get checked out in the city.

FREE **HEALTH** CLINICS

Houston Department of Health and Human Services

The Houston Department of Health and Human Services is a good first stop when you're trying to locate health services in your area. Here's a list of some of the offerings under the department's umbrella. For more information call (713) 794-9320 or visit www.houstontx.gov/health.

For Primary Care Services:

Casa de Amigos, 1809 N. Main St., (713) 236-7229
El Centro de Corazon, 7037 Capitol St., (832) 494-1610
Good Neighbor Healthcare Center, 190 Heights Blvd., (713) 529-3597
Legacy at Lyons, 5602 Lyons Ave., (713) 671-3041
South Central Houston Community Health Center, 3315 Delano St., (713) 831-9663

For Preventative Services:

South Central Houston Community Health Center, 3315 Delano St., (713) 831-9663
Casa de Amigos, 1809 N. Main St., (713) 236-7229
Legacy at Lyons, 5602 Lyons Ave., (713) 671-3041
Magnolia Health Center, 7037 Capitol St., (713) 928-9800
Northside Health Center, 8504 Schuller Rd., (713) 696-5900
Sunnyside Health Center, 9314 Cullen Blvd., (713) 732-5000
Sharpstown Health Services, 6201 Bonhomme Rd., (713) 780-5600

Ben Taub General Hospital
1504 Taub Loop
(713) 873-2000
www.hchdonline.com

Located in the Texas Medical Center, Ben Taub is home to one of the busiest trauma centers in the country, seeing more than 100,000 emergency patients every year. It is also the only hospital in Houston with a twenty-four-hour psychiatric emergency room. It is owned and operated by the Harris County Hospital District and offers a variety of free services.

FREE & CHEAP SUPPORT & TREATMENT SERVICES

Alcoholics Anonymous
(713) 686-6300
www.aahouston.org

Offers assistance to men and women dealing with alcoholism through more than 2,000 meetings a week in the Houston area. The group's telephone number is answered twenty-four hours a day, and meetings are held at 6:30 a.m. and run as late as 11 p.m.

Interfaith Ministries for Greater Houston
3217 Montrose Blvd.
(713) 533-4900
www.imgh.org

Cheap Medical Center Accommodations
Searching for discounted lodging near the Texas Medical Center? Consider checking in with area RV parks, which frequently offer discounted rates for Texas Medical Center patients. **Almost Heaven**, 4202 Del Bello Rd. in Manvel, is one such place. Call (281) 489-8561 or visit www.almostheavenrvresort.com for details.

This centrally located nonprofit organization coordinates programs such as Meals on Wheels, refugee services, disaster relief and recovery efforts, and interfaith relations in an effort to bring people with varied backgrounds and beliefs together. Check the website for more information or to get involved.

Salvation Army Greater Houston Command
1500 Austin St.
(713) 752-0677
www.salvationarmyhouston.org

Sure, you know about the Salvation Army, but are you aware of all of the services that this famous nonprofit organization offers? They include Boys and Girls Clubs, drug and alcohol rehabilitation, disaster services, shelter services, senior programs, Upward Bound for low-income families, social services, and holiday activities, most of which are free.

Star of Hope Mission
6897 Ardmore St.
(713) 748-0700
www.sohmission.org

Aiming to create a Christ-centered community that caters to Houston's homeless population, Star of Hope Mission offers various helpful programs such as a men's development center, women and families emergency shelter, women and families transitional living, homeless transitional housing, teen programs, and more. Most are free or offered for a nominal fee. Check the website for specifics.

Victory Family Outreach Ministries
222 Royder St.
(713) 699-4357
www.victoryfamilycenter.org

Anyone who has dealt with addiction knows the ways in which it can break a family apart. Add to that a financial burden and you're looking at immeasurable stress for everyone involved. That's where Victory Family Outreach Ministries comes in. By offering a recovery program that's free to participants, Victory Family eliminates the money aspect and allows those who join to focus on healing themselves and their families.

FITNESS:
WORKING IT OUT

*"I really don't think I need buns of steel.
I'd be happy with buns of cinnamon."*

—ELLEN DEGENERES

OK, I know you're probably thinking that getting a low-cost workout is a no-brainer. After all, you can throw on a pair of running shoes and hit the pavement any day of the week with no fee at all. But this is Houston, where it feels like a sauna outside for most of the year. If you prefer suffering through the heat in the company of others or staying indoors, where the sweet nectar of air-conditioning will soothe your heart-pounding soul, have no fear. Houston is filled with free and cheap exercise options for workout buffs of all types. Here are some classes, groups, and clinics that'll help you stay in tip-top shape in mind, body, and budget. The schedules sometime change, however, so be sure to verify the information on your own before you go.

BREAK **A** SWEAT **WITHOUT** BREAKING **THE** BANK

These locations offer free or cheap workout classes:

FOR FREE

Devanand Yoga Center
6423 Richmond Ave.
(713) 965-9642
www.houstonyoga.org

Regular yoga classes at Devanand Yoga Center are $15 a session, but you can apply for a yoga scholarship in exchange for volunteering that will get you into all the classes you want for free. College students are eligible for a 20 percent discount, and all newcomers receive the first week free. Print coupons from the website before you visit.

Discovery Green
1500 McKinney St.
(713) 400-7336
www.discoverygreen.com

This urban park downtown offers free group fitness classes several times a week. On Tues, you'll find PiYo, an hour-long Pilates and yoga combination class that will help you center yourself in the heart of the city. On Wed, get your groove on with Zumba, a Latin dance workout led by Oscar Sajche that promises to melt the pounds away. Both classes start at 6:30 p.m. and are held at the Anheuser-Busch Stage.

Houston Area Boot Camp
LaCenterra at Cinco Ranch
(713) 858-4397
www.houstonareabootcamp.com

Seeking a high-impact workout? Try a free Women's Adventure Boot Camp class every Wed at LaCenterra at Cinco Ranch. The class, offered by Houston Area Boot Camp, includes a challenging mix of cardio and strength training intended to tone your body while helping you lose weight. You may need to hit up Starbucks beforehand, though, as the class starts promptly at 5 a.m.

Jewish Community Center Houston
5601 S. Braeswood Blvd.
(713) 729-3200
www.jcchouston.org

The Catch: You must be a member to enjoy free classes.

The JCC's updated fitness center offers amenities such as personal TVs, free weights, a personal Pilates studio, and an indoor cycling studio, as well as a host of fun classes that make it a great alternative to a regular gym experience. Class offerings include Zumba, Pilates, spinning, water fitness, ab workouts, teen boot camp, and more. Free babysitting is also offered. Not sure if you want to commit? Try a free two-week trial.

Joy Yoga Center
4500 Washington Ave., Suite 900
(713) 868-9642
www.joyyogacenter.com

It's one of the city's foremost yoga centers, but if you do your research you can score free classes here. One way to get in for free is to take one of the "practice facilitation" classes with an instructor in training. These classes are generally offered several times a week. The center also frequently offers pay-what-you-can classes, as well as free lectures and seminars.

Lululemon Athletica

4023 Westheimer Rd.
(713) 621-8311
www.lululemon.com/houston/highlandvillage

The place that offers you all the fashionable yoga and workout gear you can imagine ups the ante on Sunday with free in-store yoga classes at 11 a.m. Come dressed to pose, and bring a yoga mat.

Texas Rock Gym

1526 Campbell Rd.
(713) 973-7625
www.texasrockgym.com

The Catch: You must be a member to attend classes for free. For nonmembers, the fee is $10.

Even if you're not particularly fond of scaling the face of massive boulders, Texas Rock Gym probably has a class that will interest you. Classes range from tai chi to yoga to kung fu to rock climbing (duh!), and are held throughout the week. There's no need to preregister; check the website for details.

ON THE CHEAP

CrossFit Houston

716 Telephone Rd.
(713) 385-5532
http://crossfithouston.typepad.com

CrossFit is a strength and conditioning program that was initially popular among police and military academies and has now become a mainstream form of exercise. Houston CrossFit typically charges $20 for a drop-in class (less if you buy a package of lessons) and offers free classes sometimes as well. Check the website for details.

Houston Arboretum and Nature Center

4501 Woodway Dr.
(713) 681-8433
www.houstonarboretum.org

The Houston Arboretum and Nature Center, a 155-acre nonprofit urban nature sanctuary, offers a variety of fitness classes including tai chi, yoga, and trail trekking. Classes are held weekly and are about $10 to $15 a session, but are discounted for members or for those who book in advance.

Night Club Cardio
Rich's, 2401 San Jacinto St.
(832) 466-1406
www.nightclubcardio.com

If you tend to prefer gin and tonics to Gatorade, here's a chance to get a workout in a setting that will be more than familiar to you: a night club. Night Club Cardio is an exercise class that uses choreographed dance moves and loud music to make you forget that you're doing something good for your body. The best part? If you register online in advance, it's just $6 a session. Sessions are held from 6:30 to 7:30 p.m. every Wed. The group also frequently offers free promotional classes—check the website for details.

Sheila Kelley S Factor
2901 W. Loop South
(713) 621-9111
www.sfactor.com

Keeping with the theme of unconventional workouts, Sheila Kelley S Factor gives adventurous women the opportunity to swap running shoes for stilettos as they test their muscles and endurance during an intense pole-dancing workout. The classes, which combine elements of ballet, yoga, and striptease, are offered in eight-week sessions. In addition to package discounts, participants receive a $40 credit for each person they refer.

Studio Nia Moves
508 Pecore St.
(713) 864-4260
www.niamoves.com

This nontraditional fitness studio offers classes ranging from belly dancing to hoop dancing to mommy-and-me workouts. The first two weeks are free, and after that packages are offered for about $10 a class. You can also get an introductory package that gets you thirty days worth of classes for $30. Family and yearly unlimited passes are also available. Free babysitting is provided for certain classes.

- **Tropa Zumba**
5110-B Ashbrooke Dr.
(713) 927-8301
www.tropazumba.com

Love Zumba? Here's your chance to try out unlimited Zumba classes for $55 a month. Classes include various types of Zumba, such as Zumba toning and Aqua Zumba. The first class is free.

GROUP **THERAPY**

Even if you're not looking to get a workout in a classroom setting, it's always fun to have a little camaraderie as you pant and wheeze your way toward your personal fitness goal. If you play well with others, here are some groups you might like to check out.

Bikesport
2909 Joanel St.
(713) 850-0250
http://bikesport.com

On Wednesday evenings, Bikesport hosts free 20- to 25-mile rides that leave at 6 p.m. from the shop. Helmets are required, and lights are recommended. All fitness levels are invited. Call for more details.

Houston Fit
Memorial Park
http://houstonfit.com

This popular half-marathon and marathon training program will get you ready for your next endurance event. The cost is $120 for twenty-nine weeks; participants also receive discounts at local sporting goods stores.

Houston Hash House Harriers
(713) 425-4274
www.h4.org

The Catch: You must be at least twenty-one to participate.

If you're the type who enjoys the occasional jog, then you'll want to check out this unique gang, which calls itself "a drinking group with a running problem." Every Sunday, the Houston Hash House Harriers take a 3- to 6-mile run that starts out with secret directions given on a special hotline and ends at an undisclosed location where kegs of beer await. It's like a giant frat party/scavenger hunt for athletic types. And it's free.

The Kenyan Way
Meets at Jackson Hill and Memorial Drive
www.kenyanway.com

Thinking of training for a marathon or half-marathon? The Kenyan Way offers twenty-five- to thirty-eight-week programs that will get you in shape to run your first long-distance event. Cost starts around $130 for a twenty-five-week course; the drop-in rate is $5.

Kicks Indoor Soccer
611 Shepherd Dr.
(713) 426-1107
www.kicksindoor.com

While the focus here is definitely soccer, Kicks offers a variety of other sports including lacrosse, ultimate Frisbee, kid's camps, roller derby, and more. The best part? If you sign up to be a member or put your kids in classes, you get to use the on-site gym for free. Two-week free trials are available for the gym. Fees for soccer and other sports vary. Check the website for details.

Luke's Locker
LaCenterra at Cinco Ranch
(281) 391-7880
www.lukeslocker.com

Every Thursday Luke's Locker in LaCenterra offers a fun run and morning social. Meet at 5:15 a.m. for the run, followed by complimentary bagels, coffee, and juice. The time may change—call ahead to confirm.

Stone Moves Indoor Rock Climbing
6970 FM 1960 Rd. West
(281) 397-0830
www.stonemoves.com

After 5 p.m. on Wednesday nights, rock climbers receive two-for-one prices for climbing (gear rentals not included). Private lessons, classes, and camps are also available.

Viking Archery
9701 Honeywell St.
(713) 771-1281

Ever wanted to shoot a bow and arrow, Robin Hood style? You can do just that for just $5 an hour at Viking Archery, which offers a full archery range as well as equipment rentals and sales. Just make sure you keep your eye on the bull's-eye—this place can draw a distractingly large crowd.

West End Bicycles
5427 Blossom St.
(713) 861-2271
www.westendbikes.com

West End Bicycles offers weekly rides at 6 p.m. on Tues and 6:30 p.m. on Thurs and a "Taco Ride" every Sun at 7:30 a.m. Ride paces vary. Call for details.

LET'S **GET** CLINICAL

From changing a flat tire to going kayaking for the first time, there's a lot to be said for free educational clinics. You can learn a lot, score some free snacks, and meet some nice folks, all in one spot. Here are some stores and venues that regularly offer free educational sports clinics.

Bike Barn
Multiple Houston locations
(713) 529-9002
www.bikebarn.com

This popular specialty bike shop offers monthly maintenance clinics at several of its locations. Clinics touch on issues including repairs, preventative maintenance, shifting, braking, and changing a flat tire.

Greater Houston Off-Road Biking Association

www.ghorba.org

The Catch: The clinics are only free for members.

Several times a year GHORBA offers public mountain-biking clinics that will teach you everything you need to know before going out to hit the trails. Check the website for details.

REI

7538 Westheimer Rd.
(713) 353-2582
www.rei.com

The Catch: Spaces fill up fast.

REI is an outdoorsy person's Mecca, and area stores offer regular free clinics on favorite activities such as kayaking expeditions, rock climbing, and adventure racing. Sign up in advance. A second location is at 17717 Tomball Parkway (832-237-8833).

Sugar Land Ice & Sports Center

16225 Lexington Blvd., Sugar Land
(281) 265-7465
http://sugarlandice.com

This popular ice rink offers a variety of hockey and figure skating lessons and clinics aimed at everyone from children to women to expert skaters. Clinics start around $5. Check the website for details.

MAKE A SPLASH

Like swimming but hesitant to fork over the bucks needed to join a master's program or country club? Here are some places where you can swim for free or a nominal fee.

Dad's Club

1006 Voss Rd.
(713) 461-6533
www.dadsclub-swimteam.com

The Catch: A facility membership is required.

This sprawling complex offers recreational swimming as well as lessons and swim teams. Monthly dues start around $40.

Fleet Aquatic Center

14654 Spring Cypress Rd., Cypress
(281) 376-2372
www.fleetswimming.com

On weekdays you can swim at this Olympic-size outdoor pool between 11 a.m. and 2 p.m. for $4 a swim. And if you decide you love it, the center also offers swim teams, lessons, and a master's program, for a monthly fee.

Memorial Park Swimming Pool

5402 Arnot St.
(713) 672-5859
www.houstontx.gov/parks

The Catch: The pool is open only from Memorial Day to Labor Day.

This 33-meter outdoor pool inside Houston's most popular park is open for lap swimming daily during the summer months. Admission is free.

Rice University

6100 Main St.
(713) 348-4058
www.ruf.rice.edu/~ricerec/aquatics

The Catch: Recreation Center memberships are typically open only to Rice faculty members and students, but throughout the year open memberships may become available. Check with the center for details.

The new 50-meter pool at the Barbara and David Gibbs Recreation and Wellness Center offers open swim as well as lessons, youth swim teams, and a master's program.

SHOPPING:
BARGAIN BASEMENT

"Whoever said money can't buy happiness simply didn't know where to go shopping."

—BO DEREK

If you're an enthusiastic shopper, there's nothing like finding a great deal, from half-price Manolos to a gorgeous vintage dress to a stunning pair of cheap earrings. Houston is a fashion Mecca, so you can be sure that when you go shopping here, you can find something for every budget. If you're willing to stray from the Galleria, you can save some major cash. Here are some of the best places to find a bargain.

THRIFT STORES

Buffalo Exchange
1618 Westheimer Rd.
(713) 523-8701

This is one of my all-time favorite stores, not only because they have a fantastic selection of secondhand goods including designer jeans and shoes and adorable vintage dresses, but also because if you play your cards right, you can walk out with a fistful of cash. In addition to selling clothes, Buffalo Exchange buys clothes, too. Bring in all of your closet casualties, hand them over to your friendly clerk, and pretend not to watch as they pore over your sacred possessions. For every item they think they can sell, you'll receive your choice of getting cash back or store credit. Pretty great, right? If you do it correctly, you can shop here and never spend a cent. A second location is at 249 W. 19th St. (713-868-2400).

Cottage Thrift Shop
811 Westheimer Rd.
(713) 526-4663
www.thewomenshome.org

If you like shopping for a good cause, this is the place. This resale shop benefits The Women's Home, which provides a safe haven for women in crisis, in a variety of ways. In addition to being an on-the-job training facility for residents who are looking for work, proceeds also provide nearly 20 percent of the home's operating income. The shop sells a variety of goods including clothing, furniture, books, and household goods.

Replay
373 W. 19th St.
(713) 863-9344

Nestled inside the Heights shopping district is this store, which has gorgeous, authentic pieces (think pillbox hats, chunky wedges, and taffeta dresses) like nothing else you've seen before. If you want to look like one of the stars of *Mad Men* in something that's authentic quality but not crazy expensive, this is the place for you.

Retropolis
321 W. 19th St.
(713) 861-1950

Want to go somewhere with a little bit of everything? This is the place to come, as you may walk out with anything from a vinyl record to a lamp shade to a vintage T-shirt. It's located in the trendy Heights shopping area and is a favorite among regulars for its eclectic collection.

Sand Dollar Thrift Store
1903 Yale St.
(713) 923-1461

I got my first introduction to this store one December, when I went in frantically searching for something to wear to a "tacky Christmas sweater party" that evening. I found a sweater (covered in awesome sequined nutcrackers, no less) and a ton of other great items. Be warned: There is a considerable amount of junk here, but if you really look, you'll find some good stuff.

Taxi Taxi Clothing
1657 Westheimer Rd.
(713) 528-5500

Coming here is kind of like going on a treasure hunt. If you're willing to take the time, you can find some wonderful pieces. Despite being at times cluttered and difficult to navigate, Taxi Taxi does have some great deals, with many vintage pieces in the $10 to $30 range. The high-heel selection here is particularly impressive. And don't miss the weekend sidewalk sales, where everything outside is just $1. Sure, there's a lot of junk mixed in, but if you dig in, you'll find something that's worth a buck.

Texas Junk Company

215 Welch St.
(713) 524-6257

You can't be a good Texan without cowboy boots, and if you're looking for a great used pair, there's no better place than the Texas Junk Company, which is home to more than 1,000 pairs of boots. From simple brown to rainbow colored, you have your pick, with some starting as low as $20. You'll also find plenty of other objects here, such as antique china, vinyl records, ashtrays, and frames. The store is open select days of the week; call for details. Cash or check only.

ANTIQUES **SHOPS**

Antique Pavilion

2311 Westheimer Rd
(713) 520-9755
http://theantiquepavilion.com

This shop is home to more than ninety dealers who offer their wares inside a 2,300-square-foot building. Offerings range from fine art to high-end jewelry, so you'll need some dough if you want to buy, but even if you can't afford it, it's always fun to go in and look at all the beautiful pieces.

B. J. Oldies Antique Shop

1435 Westheimer Rd.
(832) 651-8477
www.bjoldiesantiqueshop.com

Rather than your standard tables, chairs, and desks, this fun antiques shop specializes in interesting items such as stained glass, jewelry, and old magazines. You'll recognize the place by the herd of colorful metal animals out front. Don't see what you're looking for? Go ahead and ask—you never know what might be hiding right behind the door.

The Harwin Shopping District

If you're looking for the best deals, most insiders will point you in the direction of the Harwin Shopping District, which is located off Harwin Drive between Beltway 8 and US 59. But while it may be best known for its discount (both real and fake) designer purses, perfume, sunglasses, and watches, it's also home to some amazing clothing shops and ethnic grocery stores. Take an afternoon and walk the shops. You'll be surprised by what you find.

FlashBack Funtiques

1627 Westheimer Rd.
(713) 522-7900
www.flashbackfuntiques.net

The name pretty much says it: These antiques are also fun! If you're in the market for spaceship-shaped gumball machine, an antique Hamilton Beach mixer, or a Big Boy statue, you're in luck. The store is great for fun gift items and for collectors, and anyone visiting the Westheimer shopping block should stop in here.

Queens Furniture

7426 Harwin Dr.
(713) 784-8482
www.queensfurniture.net

This furniture store claims to offer "antiques of tomorrow" with handcrafted items including dressers, tables, chairs, desks, sofas, beds, and more. Pieces are well made and beautiful, but the best part is the prices, which tend to be considerably lower than those at other fine furniture stores in town.

Westheimer Flea Market

1731 Westheimer Rd.
(713) 874-1020
www.westheimerfleamarket.com

Located inside a former Laundromat built in 1929, this antiques shop has been selling great furniture, signs, glassware, and other goods for the past forty years. Most items are reasonably priced; if it's too expensive, try haggling. And if you haven't been in a while, give it a try. New items are always popping up.

FLEA **MARKETS**

Flea markets may have a derogatory name, but in Houston, there are lots featuring wonderful deals, eclectic crowds, and delicious food. Here are a few to consider.

The Armadillo Flea Market Mall
431 E. Airtex Dr.
(281) 443-6723
www.shoparmadillo.com

Calling itself a "merchant's bazaar," this market is pretty new to the scene and offers a selection of goods such as furniture, jewelry, food, electronics, perfumes, books, and more. It's open from 11 a.m. to 7 p.m. Thurs through Sun.

Sunny Flea Market
8705 Airline Dr.
(281) 445-1981
www.sunnyfleamarket.com

With more than 1,000 shops, this is one of the largest flea markets in the nation, featuring goods ranging from fruits and vegetables to sombreros to electronics. It's also a wonderful place to go for a meal, thanks to the stands selling delicious corn *elote,* fajitas, and shaved ice. The flea market is open every weekend.

Traders Village Houston
7979 N. Eldridge Parkway
(281) 890-5500
www.tradersvillage.com

One of the best known flea markets in town, Traders Village is a fun place to shop for gifts, arts and crafts, and holiday items. Located on more than a hundred acres, there's a little bit of something for everyone at this venue. Don't miss the special events, such as powwows, barbecue cook-offs, swap meets, and more. Traders Village is open every weekend.

SECTION 3:

Exploring Houston

CULTURE VULTURES:
THE MUSEUM DISTRICT

"Look, it's my misery that I have to paint this kind of painting, it's your misery that you have to love it, and the price of the misery is $1,350."

—MARK ROTHKO

There are few things Houstonians are more proud of than their museums. After all, from the world-renowned Menil Collection to the T. rex–inhabited Museum of Natural Science to the quirky yet fascinating National Museum of Funeral History, this town has all of its artistic bases covered. Even better, many of these museums are located in a lush, tree-lined, walkable area bordering downtown Houston. With just a little research, you can walk these hallowed corridors without shedding a single dollar from your pocket. From always-free institutions to places with discounts certain nights of the week, there's a way to navigate this scene while sticking to your budget. After all, you should be expanding your cultural horizons—not your bank statement.

ALWAYS **FREE**

ArtCar Museum
140 Heights Blvd.
(713) 861-5526
www.artcarmuseum.com

Houston celebrates artists of every type during its annual Art Car Parade, in which people decorate their cars in every material imaginable and then parade them through downtown Houston. Even if you can't make the parade (which is typically held in May), you can still get a taste of the festivities at the ArtCar Museum, which is free and open from 11 a.m. to 6 p.m. Wed through Sun. The museum features a variety of exhibits including real art cars and works by local, national, and international artists. Founded in 1998, the museum aims to offer a forum for little-known artists while celebrating the postmodern age of car culture. Even the building exterior itself is a work of art, covered in chrome and scrap metal.

Blaffer Art Museum
120 Fine Arts Building
at the University of Houston
(713) 743-9521
www.class.uh.edu/blaffer

With its mission of furthering the careers of emerging, mid-career, and under-represented artists, it seems fitting that this little museum is located on a university campus. The focus here is contemporary art, as shown through exhibits, public lectures, artists' talks, docent tours, audio guides, and youth programs. Recent exhibitions have included work from Gabriel Kuri, Amy Patton, Johan Grimonprez, and Okay Mountain. A variety of fun, hands-on programs are also available. The museum is open from 10 a.m. to 5 p.m. Tues through Sat. All exhibitions are free.

Contemporary Arts Museum
5216 Montrose Blvd.
(713) 284-8250
www.camh.org

This nonprofit institution, founded in 1948, is dedicated to serving as a forum for the best international, national, and regional art through exhibitions, lectures, programs, special events, and more. And thanks to its very generous donors, admission is always free. One of the most recognizable buildings in Houston because of its stainless steel facade, it's a must visit during a day of museum hopping in the arts district. The museum is open 11 a.m. to 7 p.m. on Wed, 11 a.m. to 9 p.m. on Thurs, 11 a.m. to 7 p.m. on Fri, and 11 a.m. to 6 p.m. Sat through Sun.

The Heritage Society
1100 Bagby St.
(713) 655-1912
www.heritagesociety.org

The Catch: The museum gallery is free, but historical house tours are $10 for adults and $8 for seniors sixty-five and over. Children eighteen and younger are free.

This museum complex, located at Sam Houston Park, is composed of a museum gallery and a variety of historic buildings including the oldest surviving brick house in Houston, a country church built in 1891, and a log cabin that dates to the 1820s. Rotating exhibits may be found at the museum on topics such as vintage postcards from the city. The museum is open from 10 a.m. to 4 p.m. Tues through Sat and from 1 to 4 p.m. on Sun. House tours are available at 10 and 11:30 a.m. and 1 and 2:30 p.m. Tues through Sat and at 1 and 2:30 p.m. on Sun. Reservations are encouraged.

Holocaust Museum Houston
5401 Caroline St.
(713) 942-8000
www.hmh.org

At once unique, sobering, and fascinating, the Holocaust Museum Houston is good reminder of why it's important to remember our past. Filled with artifacts, film reels, photographs, and text panels from the Holocaust, the museum aims to educate students and the public about the dangers of prejudice and hatred in society. Must-see artifacts at the museum include a World War II railcar similar to what was used to transport millions of people to their deaths; a Danish rescue boat that was used to save more than 7,000 people from execution; and the Eric Alexander Garden of Hope, which is dedicated to the memory of the 1.5 million children who died in the Holocaust. The museum is open from 9 a.m. to 5 p.m. Mon through Fri, noon to 5 p.m. Sat through Sun, and from 5 to 8 p.m. the first Thurs of every month. Guided tours are also available.

• Houston Center for Contemporary Craft
4848 Main St.
(713) 529-4848
www.crafthouston.org

This nonprofit center aims to educate the public about the process, product, and history of craft, particularly objects made of fiber, metal, glass, clay, and wood. How that translates to the visitor is a museum filled with cool exhibitions on topics such as paper clothing, handcrafted dolls, and jewelry made from household items. The museum is also home to the Asher Gallery, where you can shop for unique gifts created by local and national artists. Craft workshops are also available. The center is open from 10 a.m. to 5 p.m. Tues through Sat and some Sundays; call ahead to check.

• Houston Center for Photography
1441 W. Alabama St.
(713) 529-4755
www.hcponline.org

Founded in 1981, this nonprofit center aims to increase the public's appreciation of photography and its role in everyday life by working with artists and community organizations to create exhibits that will resonate with visitors.

In addition to exhibits, workshops and courses are also available on topics such as architecture photography, buying a digital camera, portraiture, and scanning tips. The center is open 11 a.m. to 5 p.m. on Wed and Fri, 11 a.m. to 9 p.m. on Thurs, and noon to 6 p.m. on Sat and Sun.

The Jung Center of Houston
5200 Montrose Blvd.
(713) 524-8253
www.junghouston.org

This nonprofit educational institution offers everything from classes to workshops to community outreach, but for art lovers, the real draw is its impressive gallery, which regularly displays the works of established and emerging artists. It is open from 9 a.m. to 7 p.m. Mon through Thurs, 9 a.m. to 4 p.m. on Fri, and 10 a.m. to 4 p.m. on Sat. Interested in submitting to the gallery? Check the website for guidelines.

Lawndale Art Center
4912 Main St.
(713) 528-5858
www.lawndaleartcenter.org

Lawndale Art Center was founded in 1979 to provide an alternative art space for a variety of artists, with an emphasis on those from the Houston area. Today, the center has four galleries that feature work by nearly 500 artists each year. On any given day, displays here may range from paintings to sculptures to photography to abstract art. Don't miss the annual Big Show, which is held in the summer and features work from emerging and under-represented Houston artists. The center is open from 10 a.m. to 5 p.m. Mon through Fri and noon to 5 p.m. on Sat; closed on Sun. Admission is free.

• Menil Collection
1515 Sul Ross St.
(713) 525-9400
www.menil.org

Perhaps the most famous museum in Houston, this collection once belonged to Houston philanthropists John and Dominique de Menil. The main collection includes work by artists such as Paul Klee, René Magritte, Joan Miró, Vincent Van Gogh, Georges Seurat, Odilon Redon, Paul Cézanne, Henri

Matisse, and Pablo Picasso. The main building is open from 11 a.m. to 7 p.m. Wed through Sat. Other must-see features include the Cy Twombly Gallery, the Dan Flavin installation, the Byzantine fresco chapel, and a variety of other parks and outdoor sculptures. Located in the heart of Houston, this is the perfect place to spend an afternoon before catching a late dinner.

Military Museum of Texas
8611 Wallisville Rd.
(713) 673-1234
www.texasmuseum.org

This nonprofit museum collects and displays military memorabilia in an effort to educate the public about the sacrifices made by men and women serving in the military. Displays include a variety of vehicles such as an M114 armored fighting vehicle, an EVT-100 armored car, an M-151 Jeep, and a half-track personnel carrier. Other artifacts, educational films, and documents are also on display. The museum is open weekends from 8 a.m. to 6 p.m. Admission is free.

• Museum of Printing History
1324 W. Clay St.
(713) 522-4652
www.printingmuseum.org

Ever wondered where the phrase "Mind your p's and q's" comes from? Ever wanted use a nineteenth-century Colombian iron handpress? Ever wanted to roll your own print of a page from the Gutenberg Bible? Even if the answer to all of these questions is no, you should still consider a visit to the Museum of Printing History, where you'll learn more than you ever needed to know about this art form. The museum also hosts classes on subjects such as making books out of everyday items, silk-screening T-shirts and posters, making letterpress business cards, and basic book and paper repair. The museum is open from 10 a.m. to 5 p.m. Tues through Sat.

Pioneer Memorial Log House Museum

1510 N. McGregor Dr.
(713) 522-0396
www.sanjacintodrt.org/pioneer.htm

Built in 1936, this log house was created as a hospitality house for visitors coming to Houston for the Texas Centennial. Now, it serves as the home of the San Jacinto Chapter of the Daughters of the Republic of Texas and an interesting little museum. Docent-led tours are available, as are regular special exhibitions for school children and the general public. Call ahead for hours.

Rice University Art Gallery

6100 Main St.
(713) 348-6069
www.ricegallery.org

This contemporary gallery focuses on installation art, meaning that when you visit you "enter the art and move through it." Having commissioned more than forty artists since 1995 and with about 40,000 people visiting annually, the gallery has built a reputation as a place to show and be shown. All installations are fully funded, from start to finish, by Rice University. The gallery is typically open from 11 a.m. to 5 p.m. Tues through Wed, 11 a.m. to 7 p.m. on Thurs, 11 a.m. to 5 p.m. Fri through Sat, and noon to 5 p.m. on Sun. It is free and open to the public.

Rothko Chapel

409 Sul Ross St. at Yupon Street
(713) 524-9839
www.rothkochapel.org

Although it's officially part of the Menil Collection, this Houston institution deserves its own entry. Dedicated in 1971, the chapel was founded by John and Dominique de Menil and was intended as a sanctuary for people of various religious backgrounds. Created by Russian-born American painter Mark Rothko, the chapel welcomes thousands of visitors every year for everything from quiet contemplation to religious meetings to weddings. The chapel is open daily from 10 a.m. to 6 p.m., 365 days a year.

Station Museum of Contemporary Art
1502 Alabama St.
(713) 529-6900
www.stationmuseum.com

This private contemporary art museum aims to provide a forum for local, national, and international artists while encouraging public awareness of the "cultural, political, economic, and personal dimensions" of art. Expect exhibitions on a variety of topics, many of which call for an end to injustice and discrimination. The museum is open from 11 a.m. to 6 p.m. Wed through Sun; admission is free.

SOMETIMES **FREE**

Buffalo Bayou ArtPark
Sabine Street Bridge between
Allen Parkway and Memorial Drive
www.bbap-houston.org

Buffalo Bayou ArtPark is a nonprofit group that was created to fill open spaces in Houston with temporary public art and expand exhibition opportunities for local artists. Currently, it offers a rotating exhibition at the Sabine Street Bridge between Allen Parkway and Memorial Drive that features twenty to twenty-five pieces by participating artists. Proposals for this and other site-specific artwork are accepted by the group year-round.

Children's Museum of Houston
1500 Binz St.
(713) 522-1138
www.cmhouston.org
Admission is free from 5 to 8 p.m. on Thurs.

If you have any kids in your life at all, this is an absolute must-see spot. Filled with fun things to do, this place will keep little ones entertained for the better part of a day. Exhibits include Kidtropolis, a city built for kids that includes its own city hall, municipal building, mercantile center, bank, news center, market, diner, art school, and vet clinic; Matter Factory, which focuses on the properties of matter and how they interact; a Building Zone, where you can discover how buildings are constructed; and a TotSpot loaded with games and toys for the thirty-six months old and under set. The museum is open from 10 a.m. to 6 p.m. Tues through Wed, 10 a.m. to 8 p.m. on Thurs, 10 a.m. to 6 p.m. Fri through Sat, and noon to 6 p.m. on Sun; closed some Mondays. Admission is $7 for adults and children age one and older, $6 for seniors sixty-five and older, and free for children under age one. The museum is a participant in Houston CityPass, so additional discounts may be available.

• Houston Museum of Natural Science
5555 Hermann Park Dr.
(713) 639-4600
www.hmns.org
On Tues, the museum offers free admission from 2 to 8 p.m. Special exhibitions require paid admission.

This famous museum is always making waves for its impressive exhibits, which in recent times have included a stinky flower that emitted a smell similar to a corpse, a huge display of terra-cotta warriors, and a BodyWorld exhibit composed of actual human bodies. Permanent exhibits include the Paleontology Hall with a tyrannosaurus rex skeleton, the Cullen Hall of Gems and Minerals filled with more than 750 pieces, and the Cockrell Butterfly Center, where a simulated tropical rainforest—complete with a 50-foot waterfall—awaits. The museum also has an IMAX, a planetarium, an energy hall, and a Texas exhibit. It typically opens at 9 a.m.; closing time varies depending on the time of year. Admission for permanent exhibits is $15 for adults and $10 for children ages three through eleven, seniors sixty-two and older, and students. Children under three are free. Added discounts may be available with use of a Houston CityPass.

John C. Freeman Weather Museum
5104 Caroline St.
(713) 529-3076
www.wxresearch.org
Admission is free from noon to 4 p.m. on Thurs.

This museum may be small, but it packs a solid punch thanks to fun, educational exhibits on topics such as world climates, hurricanes, and tornadoes. Watch a tornado being formed in a tornado chamber, see examples of weather forecasting equipment used over the years, view classic tornado and hurricane footage, and even give your own weather report at the museum's in-house weather studio. The museum is open from 10 a.m. to 4 p.m. Mon through Sat; closed on Sun. Admission (except Thurs) is $5 for adults, $3 for students, $3 for seniors, and free for children three and under. Check the website before you go for additional discounts.

• The Museum of Fine Arts, Houston
1001 Bissonnet St.
(713) 639-7300
www.mfah.org
Admission is free on Thurs and the first Sun of every month.

This is the Taj Mahal of Houston museums, and a place that every visitor or resident should visit at least once and preferably often. The museum is filled with 63,000 works of art spanning centuries and continents, and to visit here is to be at once awed, entertained, and informed. Whether you're into Asian art, photography, fashion, Native American art, or impressionism, you'll find something that catches your fancy. The collection also includes recent acquisitions from artists such as Rembrandt van Rijn, Charles Deas, and Francois-Joseph Navez. Be sure to block out nearly a full day for your visit—you won't want to miss any of it. The museum is open from 10 a.m. to 5 p.m. Tues through Wed, 10 a.m. to 9 p.m. on Thurs, 10 a.m. to 7 p.m. Fri through Sat, and 12:15 to 7 p.m. on Sun. Admission is $7.00 for adults and $3.50 for seniors sixty-five and up, students, and children ages six through eighteen. Children five and under are free.

CHEAP ADMISSION

American Cowboy Museum
11822 Almeda Rd.
(713) 433-4441
www.americancowboymuseum.org

Located on the Taylor-Stevenson Ranch, this nonprofit museum aims to increase understanding of western heritage by focusing on the contributions of African Americans, Hispanics, Native Americans, and women. The museum places a particular emphasis on reaching out to inner-city youth who will enjoy not only the museum experience but also the peacocks and goats that wander the premises. Call ahead for admission and hours.

Bayou Bend Collection & Gardens
1 Westcott St.
(713) 639-7750
www.mfah.org/bayoubend

Part of the Museum of Fine Arts, Houston, this collection of American decorative arts dating from 1620 to 1870 is located in the former home of collector and philanthropist Ima Hogg. Although the house was not built until 1928, the rooms are reminiscent of previous eras. It was Ima Hogg's wish that "Bayou Bend may serve as a bridge to bring us closer to the heart of an American heritage which unites us," and you'll find that it does just that. The collection is open from 10 to 11:30 a.m. and 1 to 2:30 p.m. Tues through Thurs and from 10 to 11:15 a.m. Fri through Sat; sixty-minute tours are offered every fifteen minutes. Admission is $10.00 for adults, $8.50 for seniors sixty-five and up and students, and $5 for children ten through seventeen. Note: No children under ten are allowed on guided tours.

Buffalo Soldiers National Museum
1834 Southmore Blvd.
(713) 942-8920
www.buffalosoldiermuseum.com

This nonprofit museum was founded in 2000 with the mission of preserving the legacy of the African-American solider. The museum is filled with historical artifacts, prints, and memorabilia as well as videos documenting the history of the Buffalo Soldiers, a contingent of African-American men and women who fought bravely during American wars from 1866 to 1951, from the Civil War through the Korean War. The museum is open from 10 a.m. to 5 p.m. Mon through Fri and 10 a.m. to 4 p.m. on Sat. Admission is $5 for adults and $3 for students.

Czech Center Museum Houston
4920 San Jacinto St.
(713) 528-2060
www.czechcenter.org

Dedicated to sharing the Czech culture with visitors from around the world, this nonprofit arts organization located in Houston's Museum District is filled with surprising information. For example, did you know that King Wenceslas, Madeleine Albright, and Martina Navratilova are all Czech? Or that the center offers genealogy research and language classes? The museum also houses artifacts such as antique furniture from European castles, a Bohemian crystal collection, and hand-painted Moravian pottery. It's open from 10 a.m. to 4 p.m. Mon through Sat. Special events are also held throughout the year. Docent tours are $6 for adults and $3 for children.

The Health Museum
1515 Hermann Dr.
(713) 521-1515
www.mhms.org

The John P. McGovern Museum of Health & Medical Science, aka The Health Museum, sees more than 200,000 visitors annually who come for its fascinating exhibits on topics such as how the human body works, aging, and digestion. Kids in particular will love the interactive "Amazing Body Pavilion," where you can sit on a set of giant teeth, walk through a giant brain, or ride a bicycle with a skeleton. The museum is open from 9 a.m. to 5 p.m. Tues through Sat and noon to 5 p.m. on Sun. In the summer admission is free on Thursday evenings. The museum is a participant in the Houston City-Pass program, which offers discounted admission to the city's most popular attractions.

Art-Inspired Eateries

Not into the museum scene? At these restaurants you can have your culture and eat there, too, thanks to inspired, interesting decor.

Goode's Armadillo Palace

5015 Kirby Dr.

(713) 526-9700

www.thearmadillopalace.com

You may expect an armadillo theme at a place with a name like this, but what you might not expect is a 20-foot re-creation of one complete with steel-plated scales, glowing red eyes, and nostrils bigger than a rack of ribs. Inside, you'll find a great bar-restaurant with solid food and darn good live music.

The Grove

1611 Lamar St.

(713) 337-7314

www.thegrovehouston.com

Located in the heart of Houston's urban park, Discovery Green, The Grove serves as a work of art in and of itself. Made of glass, wood, and steel, the restaurant was designed to blend earthiness with sophistication, resulting in a place that feels comfortable yet classy.

La Griglia

2002 W. Gray St.

(713) 526-4700

www.lagrigliarestaurant.com

Color is the name of the game at this upscale Italian restaurant, which was designed to make you feel as if you were walking into an elegant neighborhood bistro. The brightly colored murals, decorations, and accessories immediately draw your eye, keeping you entertained.

Tacos A Go-Go

3704 Main St.

(713) 807-8226

http://tacosagogo.com

The minute you walk into Tacos A Go-Go, the brightly colored mural and artwork transport you to somewhere (Tabasco, perhaps, as the painting suggests?) south of the border. The well-endowed señorita on the wall serves as an affable hostess, and the paintings of lucha libre masks ensure no dead time in your conversation. The food here is great, too.

Tony's

3755 Richmond Ave.

(713) 622-6778

www.tonyshouston.com

One of the best upscale restaurants in Houston is gaining a reputation for something other than its food: the artwork hanging on its walls. Placing an emphasis on up-and-coming artists, Tony's has commissioned pieces for the restaurant from sculptors and painters including Robert Rauschenberg, Donald Sultan, John Palmer, and Jesús Moroles.

Houston Fire Museum

2403 Milam St.
(713) 524-2526
www.houstonfiremuseum.org

Housed in a building that was once home to Fire Station No. 7, the first fire station built in Houston after it went fully paid in 1895, the museum is now an educational place for visitors of all sizes. Exhibits include a 1937 Chevrolet pumper, an antique 1938 REO fire truck, a working pull-box that allows you to pretend to dispatch a fire crew, and a locker room filled with artifacts and documents. Guided tours are available with reservations. The museum is open from 10 a.m. to 4 p.m. Tues through Sat. Admission is $3 for adults and $2 for children, students, and seniors.

Houston Maritime Museum

2204 Dorrington St.
(713) 666-1910
www.houstonmaritimemuseum.org

Ahoy, matey! Get your sea legs ready, because this museum brings with it more than 150 ship models, 100 types of navigational instruments, and a plethora of artifacts plucked straight from the sea. This nonprofit organization aims to further maritime history with a focus on local development and offers a fun experience to sea lovers. A gift shop is also located on premises and is stocked with nautical-themed items such as a copper-plated sailing lamp, a boat-themed tape dispenser, and a gemstone globe pen set. The museum is open from 9 a.m. to 4:30 p.m. Tues through Sat. Admission is $5 for adults and $3 for children eleven and under. Group tours are also available with advance notice.

Houston Railroad Museum

7390 Mesa Dr.
(713) 631-6612
www.kingswayrc.com/gcst

Everyone from those who yearn for the days of yore to youngsters who can't get enough *Thomas the Tank Engine* will love this museum, which is run by the Gulf Coast Chapter of the National Railway Historical Society and has a nice collection of railroad cars, locomotives, and artifacts, as well as a model railroad. The museum is open most Saturdays from 11 a.m. to 4 p.m., although hours are subject to change. Typically, the museum is closed during winter. Call ahead to confirm. Admission is $5.00 for adults and $2.50 for children twelve and under. Cash and checks only.

Museum of American Architecture and Decorative Arts
7502 Fondren Rd.
(281) 649-3997
www.hbu.edu

Located inside of Houston Baptist University, this museum provides an amazing look at the social history and material culture of Texas settlers between 1830 and 1930. Using artifacts such as a wooden churn, spinning wheel, and hand-loomed bedding to set the scene, the museum aims to transport visitors to another place and time. Can't-miss exhibits include the Redwood Blank Doll Collection, which shows the evolution of play dolls using artifacts from the US and abroad; the Schissler Miniature Furniture Collection, which consists of nearly two dozen pieces of antique furniture dating to the 1800s; and the Schissler Victorian Bed Chamber, which shows what a Victorian-era bedroom may have looked like. The museum is open from 10 a.m. to 4 p.m. Mon through Sat. Admission is $6 for adults, $5 for seniors, and $4 for children under twelve.

National Museum of Funeral History
415 Barren Springs Dr.
(281) 876-3063
www.nmfh.org

Call it a morbid curiosity, but I can't help loving this crazy little museum where the motto is "Any day above ground is a good one." The museum is filled to the brim with death-related artifacts, with exhibits such as a "fantasy coffin" collection (casket shapes include a chicken, a Mercedes, and a shallot); a diorama on Civil War embalming; a re-creation of a 1900s casket factory; a restored antique carved-panel hearse; and a full-scale replica of Pope John Paul II's crypt. The museum is open from 10 a.m. to 4 p.m. Mon through Fri, 10 a.m. to 5 p.m. on Sat, and noon to 5 p.m. on Sun. Admission is $10 for adults, $9 for seniors and veterans, $7 for children under twelve, and free for children under three.

1940 Air Terminal Museum
8325 Travelair St.
(713) 454-1940
www.1940airterminal.org

Heading out of town? Why not work a museum visit in before your flight? The 1940 Air Terminal Museum is conveniently located inside William P. Hobby Airport and spotlights civil, general, and business aviation. In addition to offering exhibits, the museum is also a great spot to get a bird's-eye view of the airport's operations including a daily air show. It is operated by Houston Aeronautical Heritage Society and is open from 10 a.m. to 5 p.m. Tues through Sat and to 1 p.m. on Sun. Admission is $5 for adults and $2 for children.

Rienzi Center for European Decorative Arts
1406 Kirby Dr.
(713) 639-7800
www.mfah.org/rienzi

The Rienzi Center for European Decorative Arts, which is made up of an art collection, house, and gardens, was given to the Museum of Fine Arts, Houston, by owners Carroll Sterling Masterson and Harris Masterson III in 1997. Outside, you'll find an immaculate garden that is free and open to the public. The real treasures, however, are inside, where the extensive collection includes English furniture, Worcester porcelain, continental ceramics, metalwork and glass, and impressive paintings and sculptures from artists such as Arthur Devis, George Romney, and Joshua Cristall. Hours and admission are subject to change; call ahead for details.

OFF THE BEATEN PATH

Art Museum of Southeast Texas
500 Main St., Beaumont
(409) 832-3432
www.amset.org

With roughly 1,000 pieces of art from the nineteenth, twentieth, and twenty-first centuries, you're bound to find something you like at this museum, which focuses on American and contemporary folk art through paintings, sculptures, prints, photos, and more. Don't miss John Alexander's *The Beast,* a pastel and charcoal drawing of a crocodile traipsing among the lily pads. The museum is open from 9 a.m. to 5 p.m. Mon through Fri, 10 a.m. to 5 p.m. on Sat, and noon to 5 p.m. on Sun. Admission is free.

Fort Bend Museum
500 Houston St., Richmond
(281) 342-6478
www.fortbendmuseum.org

Exhibiting the fascinating history of Fort Bend County from 1822 to 1945, this little museum provides a cool glance at what life was like years ago. Some popular attractions within the museum include the Long-Smith Cottage, one of Richmond's oldest buildings, which has been furnished to re-create middle-class life during the mid-1800s; and the 1883 John M. Moore Home, which was built in 1883 and remodeled in a neoclassical style in the early 1900s. Visitors will also enjoy wandering the galleries, which represent events such as the 1821 settlement of Spanish Texas and show the importance of the sugar and cotton industries during the plantation period. The museum is open from 9 a.m. to 5 p.m. Tues through Fri and from 10 a.m. to 5 p.m. on Sat. Admission is $5 for adults, $4 for seniors sixty-two and over, and $3 for children ages five through fifteen. Children under five are free.

Lone Star Flight Museum
2002 Terminal Dr., Galveston
(409) 740-7722
www.lsfm.org

If you love to fly, you'll love this museum, which is home to the Aviation Hall of Fame, an aviation-themed art exhibit, and a variety of aircraft and military vehicles. Not enough speed for you? Arrange a Warbird Flight Experience on a B-17 Flying Fortress, B-25 Mitchell, an AT-6 Texan, or a PT-17 Stearman. The museum is open from 9 a.m. to 5 p.m. daily. Admission is $8 for adults and $5 for seniors sixty-five and up and children ages five through seventeen. Children under five are free.

Houston Trivia

Houston is probably even more fascinating than you think. Here are some fun facts, courtesy of the City of Houston.

• Houston is the fourth biggest city in the nation (behind only New York, Los Angeles, and Chicago), and is the largest in the southern U.S. and Texas.

• The city of Houston was founded in 1836.

• The Houston metro area covers 8,778 square miles, which is slightly smaller than Massachusetts but bigger than New Jersey.

• Houston's latitude is 29 degrees, 45 minutes north, and its longitude is 95 degrees, 22 minutes west. The *Houston Chronicle* named its entertainment magazine *29-95* for this reason.

• Houston is 43 feet above sea level.

• The three-airport system serves more than fifty-one million passengers a year, including more than seven million international travelers.

• If Houston were an independent nation, it would rank as the world's thirtieth largest economy.

• Houstonians eat out more than residents of any other city. While here, you can choose to indulge in one of the more than 11,000 eateries, ranging from award-winning and upscale restaurants to memorable deli shops.

• Houston has a theater district second only to New York City with its concentration of seats in one geographic area. Located downtown, the seventeen-block Theater District is home to eight performing arts organizations with more than 12,000 seats.

- Houston has more than 500 cultural, visual, and performing arts organizations, ninety of which are devoted to multicultural and minority arts, and is one of five U.S. cities that offer year-round resident companies in all major performing arts.

- More than ninety languages are spoken throughout the Houston area.

- Houston has professional teams representing football, baseball, men's and women's basketball, soccer, and AHL hockey.

- Houston boasts more than forty colleges, universities, and institutions—offering higher education options to suit all interests.

- Houston is home to the Texas Medical Center, the largest medical center in the world, with a local economic impact of $10 billion. More than 52,000 people work within its facilities, which encompass 21 million square feet. Altogether, 4.8 million patients visit them each year.

- Home to more than 5,000 energy related firms, Houston is considered by many as the energy capital of the world.

- Houston's economy has a broad industrial base in the energy, aeronautics, and technology industries: only New York City is home to more Fortune 500 headquarters.

Lone Star Pinball Association's Pinball Museum
35222 Hempstead Hwy., Hockley

The Catch: Visits are by appointment only. E-mail Lspa@peoplepc.com for information.

Housing the personal collection of pinball enthusiast Dan Ferguson, this neat little museum is filled with 300 pinball machines and early arcade games, some of which date back to the 1920s. Expect to find all of your favorite well-known games as well as some unknown ones that are just as fun. Want to play? Chances are good he'll let you do a round or two.

Mixon's Memories Museum
506 Virginia St., South Houston
(713) 944-1615
www.bartmixon.com/museum

Ever wanted to see the clown from Stephen King's *It* in person? What about an alien autopsy from *Men in Black 2*? Find these goodies and more at Mixon's Memories Museum, a quirky 4,000-square-foot warehouse filled with movie memorabilia created by artists Bart and Bret Mixon. The museum is open every Sunday afternoon. Call ahead for hours.

Museum of the Gulf Coast
700 Procter St., Port Arthur
(409) 982-7000
www.museumofthegulfcoast.org

It may seem like a pain to trek all the way out to Port Arthur for a museum, but if you appreciate Texas history, you can't miss this 39,000-square-foot gem that is packed with everything from sports memorabilia to a free southeast Texas–centric jukebox to a fossil dig for children. Start on the bottom floor at the exhibit about the role of the Native Americans in the Gulf Coast region and work your way upstairs to the twenty-first century. The museum is open from 9 a.m. to 5 p.m. Mon through Sat and 1 to 5 p.m. on Sun. Admission is $4 for adults, $3 for seniors sixty-two and up, $2 for children ages four through eighteen, and free for children under four.

Ocean Star Offshore Drilling Rig and Museum
Pier 19 (Harborside Drive at 20th Street), Galveston
(409) 766-7827
www.oceanstaroec.com

If you're from Texas, chances are you have at least a slight interest in oil. If that's the case, you can't miss a visit to the Ocean Star Offshore Drilling Rig and Museum, where you'll board the retired rig and wander a three-story museum filled with models and interactive displays about offshore drilling. Scale models of production platforms, drill bits, and remotely operated vehicles are also available on-site. The museum is open daily from 10 a.m. to 5 p.m. Admission is $8 for adults, $5 for seniors fifty-five and up and students seven through eighteen, and free for children under seven and military personnel.

Pearl Fincher Museum of Fine Arts
6815 Cypresswood Dr., Spring
(281) 376-6322
www.pearlmfa.org

Opened in partnership with the Museum of Fine Arts, Houston, in 2008, the Pearl Fincher Museum of Fine Arts aims to bring world-class art to northwest Houston. Housed in a former library, the museum borrows from private and public collections to offer an experience unlike anything else in the area. Recent exhibitions have included British and French portraits from a Texas collection and a display of British watercolors. The museum is open from 10 a.m. to 5 p.m. Tues through Wed, 10 a.m. to 8 p.m. on Thurs, 10 a.m. to 6 p.m. on Fri, 10 a.m. to 5 p.m. on Sat, and noon to 5 p.m. on Sun. Admission is free, although donations are appreciated.

Rosenberg Railroad Museum
1921 Avenue F, Rosenberg
(281) 633-2846
www.rosenbergrrmuseum.org

Looking for a fun day trip that won't take you too far out of town? Then choo-choo choose this museum, located in Rosenberg about thirty minutes outside of Houston. In addition to big-ticket attractions such as a restored 1879 business car, an actual railroad tower that was authorized by the Texas Railroad Commission in 1903, and a facade that looks like the original train depot, the museum also offers artifacts such as original photographs, brochures, timetables, flatware, and china. The museum is open 10 a.m. to 5 p.m. Tues through Sat and 1 to 5 p.m. on Sun. Admission is $5 for adults, $4 for seniors fifty-five and over, and $3 for children one through fourteen. Adorable conductor hats for kids cost extra.

San Jacinto Monument and Museum of History

One Monument Circle, La Porte
(281) 479-2421
www.sanjacinto-museum.org

The motto here should be "come for the monument, stay for the museum." Sure, most visitors are drawn to La Porte, located about twenty minutes outside of Houston, because of the impressive San Jacinto Monument, which at 570 feet tall is 15 feet taller than the Washington Monument. The views from the monument's observation tower are impressive, and the structure itself, which has a 125-square-foot base and a 220-ton star made of stone, steel, and concrete, is a marvel. Once you're done taking it in, don't miss the museum, which is located at the monument's base and features some incredible information about Texas's history. Artifacts include antique firearms, coins from around the world, and a clarinet carried by a Civil War soldier. The museum and monument are open from 9 a.m. to 6 p.m. daily. Admission varies depending on what you see but is almost always under $10.

Spindletop—Gladys City Boomtown Museum

University Drive and Highway 287, Beaumont
(409) 835-0823
www.spindletop.org

From its malt shop to its saloon to its blacksmith shop to its general store, Spindletop gives you the opportunity to step into another place and time. A re-created boomtown from the days when oil was first discovered, this museum is a treat for kids. And with the oil tower looming like something out of Paris, you won't soon forget your time here. The museum is open from 10 a.m. to 5 p.m. Tues through Sat and 1 to 5 p.m. on Sun. Admission is $3 for adults, $2 for seniors, and $1 for children. Call ahead for more information.

Texas Energy Museum

600 Main St., Beaumont
(409) 833-5100
www.texasenergymuseum.org

During a visit to the Texas Energy Museum, learn about everything from the mechanics of early oil well drilling to the types of objects made from oil in modern times. The interactive exhibits are particularly impressive. The museum is open from 9 a.m. to 5 p.m. Tues through Sat and 1 to 5 p.m. on Sun. Admission is $2 for adults, $1 for children six through twelve and seniors sixty-five and up, and free for children under six.

Texas Prison Museum
491 Hwy. 75 North, Huntsville
(936) 295-2155
www.txprisonmuseum.org

Ever wanted to wear prison stripes without serving any actual time? Here's your chance. At the Texas Prison Museum, which is aptly located in Huntsville, home to Texas's execution chamber, $3 will get you a photo—in prison stripes—in a re-created cell. In addition, the museum offers a fascinating glimpse at prison life, with "Old Sparky," the Texas electric chair where 361 men lost their lives; a display of confiscated weapons; and an exhibit about famous inmates such as David Crosby. The museum is open from 10 a.m. to 5 p.m. Mon through Sat and noon to 5 p.m. on Sun. Admission is $4 for adults, $3 for seniors sixty and up, $2 for children six through seventeen, and free for children under six.

Texas Seaport Museum
Located at Pier 21, Galveston
(409) 763-1877
www.galvestonhistory.org

One of the biggest draws of this museum is the *Elissa,* an 1877 tall ship that is parked right outside the building. Walk across her planks, stare up at her sails, and look out onto the ocean she sailed—it's a pretty amazing experience. Inside the museum, which is run by the Galveston Historical Foundation, continue your education by checking out exhibits on topics such as shrimping in Galveston, watching films on the history of the area, and even scanning through a computer database with the names of more than 133,000 immigrants who entered the United States through Galveston. The museum is open from 10 a.m. to 5 p.m. daily. Admission is $8 for adults, $5 for children ages six through eighteen, and free for children five and under.

ART OF THE MATTER:
GREAT GALLERIES

"Good art is in the wallet of the beholder."

—KATHY LETTE

Art is a subjective, er, subject. One person can look at a piece of art and feel as if he's staring into a glimpse of his own soul, while another can see it and feel like she could make something better at home with her daughter's Crayolas. Finding something that everyone loves would be an impossible task.

That's why Houston is a great place for art lovers.

Houston's strong art scene extends to its galleries, which are filled with interesting, educational, and sometimes just plain weird works. Even if you can't afford what's in them, galleries are a fun place to browse. After all, it's free to look. Here are some of the best galleries to check out.

Aerosol Warfare: Graffiti Art Gallery & Artists
2110 Jefferson Ave.
(832) 748-8369
www.aerosolwarfare.com

An urban art gallery and resource center, Aerosol Warfare is dedicated to furthering graffiti art through exhibitions and partnerships. Rather than resorting to areas that are inappropriate or even illegal, Aerosol Warfare wants to help graffiti artists find a place to express their unique art form. Hours can vary; check the website for details.

Anya Tish Gallery
4411 Montrose Blvd.
(713) 524-2299
www.anyatishgallery.com

Houston is a very diverse city, and this gallery aims to spotlight some of this diversity by focusing on artists from central and eastern Europe and Russia while also featuring local artists. Artwork on display includes painting, sculpture, photography, and video. The gallery is open from 10:30 a.m. to 6 p.m. Tues through Fri and 10:30 a.m. to 5 p.m. on Sat.

Archway Gallery
2305 Dunlavy St.
(713) 522-2409
www.archwaygallery.com

With a membership of thirty artists, this gallery aims to offer personalized service and attention to each of its visitors. It features sculpture, pottery, and painting in various styles. Check the ample website to see if you like any of the work, or simply stop in from 10 a.m. to 6 p.m. Mon through Sat or 1 to 5 p.m. on Sun.

Barbara Davis Galleries
4411 Montrose Blvd.
(713) 520-9200
www.barbaradavisgallery.com

Emphasizing contemporary artists, this gallery in the Montrose district has been home to work from internationally known artists such as Julie Mehretu, Mie Olise, and Shahzia Sikander. Call for hours and details.

Bering Art Collective
805 Rhode Place
(713) 524-0101
www.beringandjames.com

Talk about cool. This 3,500-square-foot space is an art lover's dream, filled with things you can imagine hanging on your walls. The art is contemporary; the gallery hosts ten to twelve exhibitions a year. Stop by weekdays between 9 a.m. and 5 p.m. to check it out.

Betz Art Gallery
1208 W. Gray St.
(713) 576-6954
www.betzgallery.com

This gallery has a little mix of everything, such as oil paintings, bronze sculptures, ceramics, and jewelry. Free events are held regularly to expose the gallery to the public; exhibitions change monthly. Call for hours and details.

Booker-Lowe Australian Art
4623 Feagan St.
(713) 880-1541
www.bookerlowegallery.com

The colors are nearly overwhelming here when you first walk in, thanks to the gorgeous variety of Aboriginal artwork. Exhibits rotate regularly and works can range from $200 to $35,000. The gallery is open from 11 a.m. to 5 p.m. Wed through Sat.

Dean Day Gallery

2639 Colquitt St.
(713) 520-1021
www.deandaygallery.com

With contemporary work from more than three dozen artists circulating through here on regular basis, this is a good place to watch if you've been thinking about getting a piece. The work here is varied but high in quality. The gallery is open from 11 a.m. to 5 p.m. Tues through Sat.

Deborah Colton Gallery

2445 North Blvd.
(713) 869-5151
www.deborahcoltongallery.com

By being open to a variety of contemporary arts, from painting to works on paper to video and photography, Deborah Colton has created an interesting, fluid space for viewing these works from international artists. The gallery is open from 10 a.m. to 5:30 p.m. Tues through Sat.

De Santos Gallery

1724 Richmond Ave.
(713) 520-1200
www.desantosgallery.com

This photography gallery places an emphasis on Spanish fine-art photography but also displays other work from local and international artists in the three-story building. The gallery is open from 10:30 a.m. to 5 p.m. Tues through Sat.

DiverseWorks Art Space

1117 East Freeway
(713) 223-8346
www.diverseworks.org

This nonprofit art center is a forum for all types of visual, performing, and literary art and frequently hosts exhibitions that it feels will resonate with the community. Check the website for upcoming events that might interest you.

Get Your Freak On: Houston's Quirky Side

Houston may be known for money, size, and smog, but it's also got a very eclectic side. Here are five such spots.

Beer Can House

222 Malone St.

(713) 880-2008

www.beercanhouse.org

Run by the ever cool Orange Show for Visionary Art, this Houston land-mark/work of art/house made of beer cans(!) is a famous example of the city's innovate art scene. Originally nothing more than one dude's hobby (most of the beers displayed are types owner John Milkovisch likes to drink), the house is now adorned with an estimated 50,000 cans. It's just something, frankly, you need to see for yourself. The house is open from noon to 5 p.m. Sat and Sun; admission is $1.

Caroline Collective

4820 Caroline St.

(832) 429-6867

http://carolinecollective.cc

OK, so this place isn't really weird so much as it's cool. Caroline Collective is a "coworking community" where people who don't want to work in an office environment but also don't want to work at home can come to con-duct their day-to-day operations. Not only that, but it's run by the city's social media cool kids, meaning you're always in good company and well positioned for conversation when you go there. They also host a variety of special events, from yoga classes to product launches to swap meets.

DeLorean Motor Company

15023 Eddie Dr., Humble

(281) 441-2537

www.delorean.com

Here's a little-known fact about Houston: We've got our own branch of the DeLorean Motor Company. (Hopefully you remember the two-door auto from *Back to the Future*?) And if you call ahead, they'll give you a tour of the factory. Even though the car is no longer made, there are still a decent number of DeLoreans out there, and they need servicing, which is why the branch is still around. And if you decide you're ready to purchase, they can help you with that, too. But be warned: They typically run around $40,000.

501st Legion, Star Garrison

www.stargarrison.com

File this one under awesome: It's a group of adults who dress up in Star Wars garb and show up at charity events for kids. The group celebrates the "Star Wars universe" while contributing to the local community, and these guys and gals take their work seriously, from wearing authentic-looking costumes, to making a point to be on time, to participating in charitable functions. Want to get be a Vader, Leah, or Jabba (or have the group come out to your event)? Check the website for details.

Project Row Houses

2521 Holman St.

(713) 526-7662

www.projectrowhouses.org

Project Row Houses started in 1993, when an artist and activist in Houston's underserved North Third Ward named Rick Lowe decided to turn an abandoned row of twenty-two shotgun-style houses into an artists' enclave. Since then, the project has expanded to include forty properties. In addition to offering an outlet for artists, Project Row Houses also focuses on other important issues such as neighborhood revitalization, low-income housing, historic preservation, and community service. Exhibits are held in houses throughout the year. Call or check the website for specifics.

Rebel's Honky Tonk

5002 Washington Ave.

(713) 862-7172

www.rebelshonkytonkhouston.com

Urban Cowboy fans who visit Houston tend to have one question in particular: Is there a mechanical bull somewhere we can ride? For a long time the answer was no. But thanks to Rebel's Honky Tonk, a glossy new dance hall on Washington Avenue, there is once again a place to get down and dirty on a motor-operated cow. And with free mechanical bull rides at least a portion of every night they're open (Wed through Sat), you can get into the groove without spending a cent. Great happy hour deals (including free draft beer if you sing karaoke on Wed) are also available.

18 Hands Gallery
249 W. 19th St.
(713) 869-3099
www.18handsgallery.com

If you like ceramic art, you'll enjoy a walk through this space, which features monthly exhibits as well as work from more than forty-five clay artists. One of the few places showcasing fine ceramic art in the city, the space feels professional but approachable. The gallery is open from 10 a.m. to 6 p.m. Wed through Sat and noon to 5 p.m. on Sun.

Gallery Sonja Roesch
2309 Caroline St.
(713) 659-5424
www.gallerysonjaroesch.com

Aiming to counter the "visual overload" the art world is experiencing, Sonja Roesch designed this gallery to focus on concept-based art that incorporates color, light, and alternative materials to keep the works fresh and interesting. It's not for everybody, but it's definitely an innovative space. The gallery is open from 11 a.m. to 6 p.m. Tues through Sat.

Gittings Portraiture
1121 Uptown Park Blvd.
(713) 965-9301
www.gittings.com

Know someone who's always wanted to see a pop-art version of themselves? This is the place to get it. At Gittings, you can get your picture taken and pick up an Andy Warhol–esque reproduction of it a few weeks later. Not into that? It's still worth a visit to the gallery, which is filled with gorgeous photography. Call for hours.

H Gallery
617 W. 19th St.
(713) 456-9513
www.hgallery.org

By focusing on local artists, H Gallery has created an innovative space for anyone interested in the Houston art scene. Navigating the gallery can be a little like going on a treasure hunt at times, but treasures you will find thanks to the wide selection here. The gallery is open from noon to 7 p.m. Fri through Sun.

Hanh Gallery
2800 Kirby Dr.
(713) 412.1771
www.hanhgallery.com

Looking for a unique piece for your living room? Houston artist Hanh Tran is known for her thick, textural oil paintings that focus on everything from animals to Texas pride to portraits. Even better? She frequently invites the public into her private studio for viewing parties that include free wine and snacks. Check the website for details and contact information.

Hooks-Epstein Gallery
2631 Colquitt St.
(713) 522-0718
www.hooksepsteingalleries.com

One of Houston's longest-running art galleries, this interesting space features work from mid-career and emerging artists as well as those who are better known while specializing in American, European, and Latin art from the nineteenth and twentieth centuries. The gallery is open from 11 a.m. to 5 p.m. Tues through Sat.

Houston Center for Contemporary Craft
4848 Main St.
(713) 529-4848
www.crafthouston.org

This nonprofit is dedicated to all forms of craft, particularly those created from materials such as fiber, metal, glass, clay, and wood, and provides a venue for local and national artists hoping to show their work. Workshops, gallery talks, studio demonstrations, and outreach programs are also available.

John Cleary Gallery
2635 Colquitt St.
(713) 524-5070
www.johnclearygallery.com

This gallery says it focuses on "good photography," and its walls are filled with just that, from antique photos to shots of Texas geography to artistic, interpretive offerings. The gallery is open from 10 a.m. to 5 p.m. Tues through Sat.

Las Manos Magicas Folk Art
4819 Blossom St.
(713) 802-2530
www.lasmanosmagicas.com

Folk art is big in Texas, and Las Manos Magicas is one of the absolute best places you can go to find it. This funky, eclectic little shop is filled with artwork from both local and international artists. If nothing else, this is a fun place to spend an hour or two browsing the very unique offerings. The gallery is open from 10:30 a.m. to 5:30 p.m. Wed through Sat.

Midtown Art Center
3414 La Branch St.
(713) 521-8803
www.midtownartcenter.com

Striving to promote art throughout Houston, the Midtown Art Center serves as both a teaching ground and exhibition space for local artists. Art here ranges from contemporary work to theater and dance performances, with an emphasis on emerging and established visual artists.

Moody Gallery
2815 Colquitt St.
(713) 526-9911
www.moodygallery.com

Opened by Betty Moody in 1975, this gallery has always placed an emphasis on work by Texas artists or people with a strong connection to Texas. All types of media are welcome here. The gallery is open from 10:30 a.m. to 5 p.m. Tues through Fri and 11 a.m. to 5 p.m. on Sat.

Nolan-Rankin Galleries
6 Chelsea Blvd.
(713) 528-0664
www.nolan-rankingalleries.com

Francophiles, rejoice! This gallery's for you. Filled with contemporary French art (as well as work from some American painters), this place overwhelms the senses with its offerings. It is open from 10 a.m. to 5 p.m. Tues through Fri and 10 a.m. to 3 p.m. on Sat.

O'Kane Gallery
One Main St. at the
University of Houston Downtown
(713) 221-8042
www.uhd.edu

The showplace at the University of Houston-Downtown features work by local artists in the areas of visual arts and contemporary culture. The gallery aims to bring in work that will be both intellectually stimulating and relevant, choosing artists it feels will make a significant impact on people who view their work. The gallery is free and open to the public. It is open from 10 a.m. to 5 p.m. Mon through Sat.

Sicardi Gallery
2246 Richmond Ave.
(713) 529-1313
www.sicardi.com

Since it opened in 1994, this gallery has made a point to use works of art to increase a dialogue between Latin America and the United States and Europe. By hosting exhibitions by Latin American artists, the gallery furthers that mission while drawing some of the most innovative artwork around. The gallery is open from 10 a.m. to 5:30 p.m. Tues through Fri and 11 a.m. to 5 p.m. on Sat.

Wade Wilson Art
4411 Montrose Blvd.
(713) 521-2977
www.wadewilsonart.com

By showcasing painters, photographers, and sculptors whose work has not been seen many other places, Wade Wilson Art provides a forum for new and lesser-known artists in Houston. Some artists he has worked with include Joseph Marioni, Danielle Frankenthal, Joseph Cohen, and Jill Moser. The gallery is open from 11 a.m. to 5 p.m. Tues through Sat.

Winter Street Studios
2101 Winter St.
(713) 862-0082
www.winterstreetstudios.net

This former furniture factory that was at one point slated for demolition has now become a convent of sorts for Houston artists. With more than seventy-five art studios within the building for more than eighty-seven local artists, the creativity practically radiates from the walls. Go to the website to see the various works and make an appointment to visit.

SPORTS:
CHEAP COMPETITION

*"On this team, we are all united in a
common goal: to keep my job."*

—LOU HOLTZ

Another major benefit to living in a city the size of Houston is that we have access to all of the best sports, from NBA to MLB to NFL (Texans, not Oilers), and ways to see them—for cheap. We've got soccer and roller derby, too. From discount tickets to stadium tours, here are the best ways to get in the game.

GOING **PRO**

Houston Aeros
1510 Polk St. (at the Toyota Center)
(713) 974-7825
www.aeros.com

I know what you're thinking: hockey in Houston? It may come as a shock, but Houston has a darn good hockey team. And because many people still don't know about them, going to a game can be a steal. General admission tickets are around $15, but if you go on a Sunday during family day, you can score four tickets, $20 in Toyota Center bucks, four Aeros gifts, free parking, and a postgame activity for the family for $65. There's also a happy hour package that costs $35 and includes a club-level ticket, $10 in Toyota Center bucks, and a drink coupon to Maple Leaf Pub. The package is available Mon through Thurs. Check the website for more deals.

Houston Astros
501 Crawford St. (at Minute Maid Park)
(713) 259-8000
www.houstonastros.com

If you want to see a professional ballgame in Houston, there's no more affordable way to do it than with an Astros game at Minute Maid Park. Special deals are offered nearly every day that will score you everything from $1 tickets to dinner and a seat for just a few bucks. Recent specials have included family days where $10 buys you a hot dog, soda, chips, and a ticket; and "double play Tuesdays," where you can trade two Powerade labels for two deck seats for $2. The park also regularly offers free family zones, bring-your-dog days, and more. Just look under the "promotions and giveaways" section of the website for the best deals. Want to see a different side of the park? Try taking one of the tours of Minute Maid Park, which are offered at 10 a.m., noon, and 2 p.m. Mon through Sat. Tours include visits to Union Station, the broadcasting booth, or press boxes, the Astros' dugout, luxury suites, and more. Early-bird tours are also offered prior to home games. Regular tour tickets are $9 for adults, $7 for seniors sixty-five and over, and $5 for kids three through fourteen. Early-bird tours cost slightly more.

Houston Dynamo
1001 Avenida de las Americas
(713) 276-7500
www.houstondynamo.com

Since Houston received its own professional soccer league a few years back, the city has worked hard to embrace it. Now, it's as much a part of the city as the Rockets, Texans, or Astros. If you haven't been yet, you have to check it out. The atmosphere is unlike any of the other major sports. And tickets are cheap, starting around $10, with discounts available online.

Houston Rockets
1510 Polk St. (at the Toyota Center)
(713) 758-7315
www.nba.com/rockets

Want to see Yao Ming, Shane Battier, Kyle Lowry, and friends shoot some hoops? You're in luck, because there are super cheap ways to see them in action. General admission tickets are generally affordable, but the best way to ensure a good deal is to sign up online for the Rockets Insider program, which gives you access to deals, news, and event sign-ups before they are available to public. Some recent deals listed in the Rockets Insider e-mail blast include guys' night out packages (two tickets, hot dogs, beers, and glasses for $50), family night out, and even an opportunity to send your sweetie a singing telegram from Rockets mascot Clutch. More interested in what happens behind the scenes? Take a backstage tour, offered from 10 a.m. to 3 p.m. Mon through Fri. You'll get to see everything from the arena floor to the artists' prep room to the super-pricey lounge and box areas. Fortunately, the tour is not super pricey, at $7 for adults and $5 for children twelve and under and for seniors sixty-five and over. Reservations are required. Note: Tours are not offered on game days.

Everyday Tourist

I've already told you about some of the behind-the-scenes stadium tours, but here are some other Houston tours that are worthy of your looking like a tourist for an hour or two.

Buffalo Bayou

Group meets at I-610 and Woodway Drive

(713) 752-0314

www.buffalobayou.org

Most people don't know that Houston has a steady stream of water, known as Buffalo Bayou, that runs straight through downtown. For a long time it seemed like the city didn't know what to do with it. Thankfully, the Buffalo Bayou Partnership came along. Now, you can take a kayak tour right down the bayou as a guide tells you all about it. Run by North Lake Conroe Paddling Company, the tours are offered from 9 a.m. to 1 p.m. several times a month and cost $60. Yes, it's a splurge, but it's a way to see Houston like never before. Register in advance—or, even better, get your own kayak, read up about the bayou on the partnership's website, and design your own tour for free. The bayou is considered an official paddling trail; visit www.tpwd.state.tx.us.

Houston Roller Derby

611 Shepherd Dr. (inside Kicks Indoor Soccer)

www.houstonrollerderby.com

OK, this one's not professional, but you'll still get some serious high-flying, high-rolling, high-speeding action. Houston has a fantastic women's roller derby team that offers bouts (that's games, to you and me) from Mar to Sept. It's family friendly, but you're also welcome to grab a beer or two as you watch these athletic speed demons with names such as Hotrod Betty,

Houston Zoo

6200 Hermann Park Dr.

(713) 533-6500

www.houstonzoo.org

One of Houston's most popular attractions offers a half-day, air-conditioned tour. Arrive at the park at 9 a.m. and make your way to the Carruth Natural Encounters Building, where you'll meet a sweet red panda named Toby. Then, you'll head to the other areas of the park, such as the reptile and amphibian house, the tropical bird house, the sea lion area, and the Kipp Aquarium. The tour includes the chance to meet the keepers of some of the animals. Call for pricing information, as it is subject to change.

The Orange Show

2402 Munger St.

(713) 926-6368

www.orangeshow.org

Known for its eccentric buildings around town, the Orange Show for Visionary Arts also offers a great series of Eyeopener tours that give you an even better feel for the eccentricity of this city. The tours, which are offered every few months, typically have different themes, such as public art in interesting places or Houston's hidden gems. Prices vary depending on the tour. Call or check the website for details.

Rebel Ann, and Dutch Destroyer try to knock each other out of the way. General tickets are $12 or $15 at the door; season tickets are $80. Want an even better deal? Volunteer and see all the games you want for free. Check the website for details.

Houston Texans

Two Reliant Park (at Reliant Stadium)

(832) 667-2000

www.houstontexans.com

No city was more excited to get an NFL team back in town than Houston, where we had gone without one for several years after the Houston Oilers moved to Tennessee. The price of general admission tickets, which start at $35, to see the Texans at Reliant Stadium is not terrible, but if you're smart about it you can get an even better deal. Discount brokers such as stubhub. com, for example, offer the same tickets for greatly discounted prices, meaning that for many games you could easily score a pair of tickets for $30. Not bad, huh? Another tip: tailgating. Tailgating in the parking lots around the stadium is a huge rite of passage for Texans, and you'd be surprised by the people you meet. They'll hand you a beer, offer you some barbecue, and might just give you a free ticket—it's happened to me.

THAT TIME OF YEAR:
ANNUAL EVENTS

"So, where's the Cannes Film Festival
being held this year?"

—CHRISTINA AGUILERA

People love festivals. From Sundance to Bonnaroo to Burning Man, there's something about annual events that we all gravitate toward. Maybe it's the high-profile artists and exhibitors. Maybe it's the grand sense of unity. Maybe it's the fried Twinkies. No matter what the draw, any great city has to have ample special events that entice locals and visitors every year.

If you live in or happen to be visiting Houston, you're in luck, because we've got a lot of world-class options that won't cost you an arm and a leg. From a fantastic art show to a funky parade of well-dressed cars to a must go for brides-to-be, you're sure to find something you'll want to do here—year after year.

JANUARY

Bridal Extravaganza Show
George R. Brown Convention Center
1001 Avenida de las Americas
(281) 340-7777
www.bridalextravaganazashow.com

Held every Jan and July, the Bridal Extravaganza Show features more than 400 wedding-related companies over two days at the George R. Brown Convention Center. There, you'll find everything from wedding boutiques that bring dresses for you to try on, to DJs broadcasting playlists, to limo services ready to take you for a ride. I went, paid the $10 admission fee, and walked out with someone to make the invitations, a free engagement photo session, and all the samples of cake I could handle. It's definitely a deal.

Chevron Houston Marathon
Course typically starts and ends at the
George R. Brown Convention Center
1001 Avenida de las Americas
(713) 957-3453
www.chevronhoustonmarathon.com

This marathon is one of the most popular in the country because the course tends to be really flat and really fast. In fact, it's become so popular that a lottery is held every Aug to determine who will be able to participate. Don't make it in? Consider volunteering or going out to cheer from the sidelines; the atmosphere the day of the race is very much that of a party.

MARCH

Azalea Trail
(713) 523-2483
www.riveroaksgardenclub.org/azaleatrail.cfm

Houston may not always be known for its beauty, but every spring parts of it become alive with color as gorgeous azaleas start to bloom. The Azalea Trail, hosted by the River Oaks Garden Club, gives participants the chance to get an up-close view of these flowers, which range in color from pink to purple to yellow, at seven area locations. The cost is typically $5 for individual sites or $15 for all locations.

Bayou City Art Festival
Held at Memorial Park, 6501 Memorial Dr.,
in March
Held downtown, 901 Bagby St.,
in October
(713) 521-0133
www.bayoucityartfestival.com

Held twice a year, this art festival draws more than 300 artists showing off work at this rainbowlike outdoor gallery. If you go, you should also know that you're benefiting a good cause: To date, the festival has donated nearly $2.5 million to local charities. Tickets are $10; free for children under twelve.

BVVA Compass Tour de Houston
(832) 393-0970
www.houstontx.gov/tourdehouston

This annual bike ride benefits the Houston Parks and Recreation Department and brings together people from all pockets of the city. Riders can choose between a 20-, 40-, or 70-mile ride that kicks off at City Hall and then winds through the town's historic districts, neighborhoods, and parks. Registration to ride is typically around $25 and benefits the Houston Parks and Recreation Department.

Donegal Beard Growing Contest at Saint Arnold Brewery
2000 Lyons Ave.
(713) 686-9494
www.saintarnold.com

What better way to spend Saint Patrick's Day weekend than drinking lots of beer and judging folks based on their beards? Each year, Saint Arnold Brewery hosts this competition, which is as simple as it sounds: Participants grow beards, then show up at the brewery on the designated day to rock their beards in front of a panel of judges as an unruly crowd cheers them on. Trust me, it's a good time. Tickets are typically around $5.

Houston Livestock Show and Rodeo
Reliant Park
8334 Fannin St.
(832) 667-1000
www.hlsr.com

One of Houston's pride and joys, this annual event draws more than two million visitors eager to try out the sights, sounds, and tastes (fried Twinkie, anyone?) that the city has to offer. Events include everything from wine tasting to silent auctions to a good old-fashioned midway. One of the hottest tickets, however, is the Rodeo Barbecue Cook Off, when hungry patrons pile into sponsored tents for free food and booze. You have to be invited to attend, so if you get an invite, go. You'll end up happy, full, and buzzed, without spending a dime. General admission rodeo and concert tickets start around $18, although discounts are available.

APRIL

Houston International Festival

Held downtown at 400 Rusk St.
(713) 654-8808
www.ifest.org

Created to celebrate diversity and the multitude of cultures that are well represented in Houston, iFest is an annual festival of food, fun, song, dance, and education about one particular country or area of the world. The festival incorporates events, history, food, and traditions from a different country each year, offering a fun experience for all types of people from the community. Past themes have included the Caribbean, the Silk Road, and Australia, to name a few. Adult tickets cost around $12.

San Jacinto Day Festival and Battle Reenactment

One Monument Circle, La Porte
(281) 479-2421
www.sanjacinto-museum.org

Who doesn't love a good re-enactment—particularly when it centers around a super-important battle in Texas history? Every Apr, during the San Jacinto Day Festival, an army of actors takes to the field to reenact the Runaway Scrape, when Texas settlers fled their homes after rebellions against the Mexican government, beginning with the siege of the Alamo in 1836 and ending with the Battle of San Jacinto. The free festival also includes music, entertainment, food, games, and other events.

MAY

Art Car Parade
(713) 926-6368
www.orangeshow.org/art-car

Perhaps Houston's most beloved festival, the annual Art Car Parade rolls through town every May, featuring more than 250 vehicles painstakingly decorated by their owners and an audience of 250,000 that comes out to enjoy the fun. Pack a cooler, arrive early, and stay until it ends: This free event, which is held along Allen Parkway, is quintessential Houston.

JULY

Houston Symphony's $1 Concert
615 Louisiana St.
(713) 224-7575
www.houstonsymphony.org

A summer tradition for more than fifty years, the Houston Symphony continues to offer its annual $1 concert, in which visitors can enjoy a symphony performance in Jones Hall for just a buck. The event also honors the first-prize winner in the Ima Hogg Young Artist Competition.

Mixers and Elixirs at the Houston Museum of Natural Science
5555 Hermann Park Dr.
(713) 639-4629
www.hmns.org

It's fun to go to the Houston Museum of Natural Science anytime, but on Fri during the summer, it's extra fun thanks to the Mixers and Elixirs event. For four hours each Fri, the museum turns into a giant party featuring live music, booze, free appetizers, and other festivities. Tickets start around $14.

AUGUST

Theater District Open House
(713) 658-8938
www.houstontheaterdistrict.org

During this annual event, members of the Theater District such as the Wortham Theater Center, Alley Theatre, Jones Hall, and the Hobby Center for the Performing Arts open their doors for free backstage tours and also offer discount tickets to their performances. The event is typically held from noon to 4 p.m.

White Linen Night in the Heights
(832) 273-4798
http://whitelinennightheights.com

For a few years now, the Heights has been one of the coolest neighborhoods in the city, filled with cafes, boutiques, and gorgeous historic housing that makes spending an afternoon there a joy. During this annual free event, members of the neighborhood celebrate its unique vibe with a festival of live music, art, food, parties, shopping, and more. The Heights also offers a First Saturday event (on the first Sat of each month) that spotlights its most interesting venues.

OCTOBER

Re/Max Ballunar Liftoff Festival
1201 Nasa Rd. 1
(281) 488-7676
www.ballunarfestival.com

If you've always wanted to ride in a hot-air balloon, the annual Re/Max Ballunar Liftoff Festival is the perfect chance to get acquainted with the giant mechanisms. Admission is just $10 a vehicle for the events, which include

hot-air balloon competitions, balloon glows, skydiving exhibitions, conces-
sions, arts and crafts, aviation equipment displays, and more.

Texas Renaissance Festival
21778 FM 1774, Plantersville
(800) 458-3435
www.texrenfest.com

Like to get your medieval on? Here's your chance. Every Oct and Nov, the
Texas Renaissance Festival jousts its way to Plantersville (located about an
hour from Houston but well worth the drive) to fill the otherwise open
spaces with beer, turkey legs, and chain mail. The characters here (paid and
otherwise) are absolutely fascinating. Events include falconry, magic shows,
juggling, rides, jousting, and shopping. Tickets start around $12.

NOVEMBER

Nutcracker Market
Reliant Center
8334 Fannin St.
(713) 535-3271
www.houstonballet.org

One of Houston's greatest holiday traditions, the Nutcracker Market (which
benefits the Houston Ballet) takes place over a long weekend every Nov
inside Reliant Center. Featuring more than 300 vendors, this is the perfect
place to get a jump on your holiday shopping. But if the shopping starts to
wear you down, don't worry—there are plenty of food and beverage options
available as well. Admission starts around $11.

Uptown Holiday Lighting
Post Oak Boulevard, between San Felipe Street and Westheimer Road
(713) 621-2504
www.uptown-houston.com

Nothing screams "it's the holidays!" better than a good tree lighting, and
if you're into that sort of thing, you can't beat the one at Uptown Park.

Featuring a half million lights, costumed holiday-themed characters, festive music, and an appearance from Santa, this is bound to get you into the holiday spirit. Held just after Thanksgiving; check the website for details. The event is always free.

DECEMBER

Dickens on the Strand
Held between 20th and 26th Streets, Galveston
(409) 765-7834
www.dickensonthestrand.com

The nineteenth century comes to life during this annual Galveston event, which re-creates the life that Charles Dickens may have lived in Victorian London. If you go, brush up on your Dickens, as characters from his novels wander the streets. Other events include strolling carolers, parades, costumed vendors, themed food, and holiday decorations and gifts. Tickets start around $9.

Heritage Society's Candlelight Tour
1100 Bagby St.
(713) 655-1912
www.heritagesociety.org

Another Houston tradition, this event takes you back to the 1800s for the holidays as costumed actors re-create what life would have been like during that time. Because the event is held in historical homes, it feels incredibly authentic—magical, even—as you walk the grounds. Traditional events, such as photos with Santa and holiday craft creations, are also available. Tickets cost around $10.

APPENDIX A:

CHEAP **ACCOMODATIONS**

When you visit a city the size of Houston, you can take your pick of lodging, from hostels to major chains to five-star hotels. Here are some of the best budget-friendly options.

HOSTELS

Want a cheap place to bunk? Here are two solid spots within walking distance of downtown and major attractions.

Friends Guesthouse and Hostel
1818 Lubbock St.
(832) 889-8411
www.friendsguesthouse.com

Located inside the 6th Ward neighborhood, this hostel manages to be both quiet and friendly. The house itself is charming, and the location offers easy access to downtown and public transportation. Rates start around $25 a night for a private room.

Houston International Hostel
5302 Crawford St.
(713) 523-1009
www.houstonhostel.com

If all you need is a basic place to lay your head, the Houston International Hostel is a nice option. Plus, its location in the Museum District can't be beat. Attractions such as Hermann Park, the Japanese Garden, the Houston Museum of Natural Science, the Museum of Fine Arts, and the Houston Zoo are within easy walking distance. Prices start around $15 a night.

SCORING **BUDGET-FRIENDLY** HOTELS

Houston is one of the country's biggest business hubs, so it only makes sense that when the business travelers flee the city on Friday afternoon, rates go down at business-centric hotels.

Here are some places where you're likely to find particularly good deals on weekends:

Aloft, 5415 Westheimer Rd., (713) 622-7010, www.alofthoustongalleria.com
Courtyard Houston Downtown, 916 Dallas St., (832) 366-1600, www.marriott.com
Crown Plaza Houston North Greenspoint, 425 N. Sam Houston Parkway East, (281) 445-9000, www.cpnorthhouston.com
Homewood Suites, 2950 Sage Rd., (713) 439-1305, www.homewoodsuites.com
Houston Marriott West Loop, 1750 W. Loop South, (713) 960-0111, www.marriott.com
Renaissance Houston, 6 Greenway Plaza East, (713) 629-1200, www.marriott.com

ON **THE** WEB

Some helpful sites for scoring travel deals in Houston:

www.airfarewatchdog.com
www.priceline.com
www.travelzoo.com
www.kayak.com
www.sidestep.com
www.tripadvisor.com
www.visithoustontexas.com

LOCAL **MEDIA**

Want the scoop on what's happening around town? Here are some good resources:

NEWS **&** ENTERTAINMENT **PUBLICATIONS**

Free Press Houston: www.freepresshouston.com
Houston Chronicle: www.chron.com
Houston Press: www.houstonpress.com
Paper City: www.papercitymag.com

ON **TV**

Great Day Houston: www.khou.com/great-day
Wild About Houston: www.houston55.com/wild-about-houston

MAGAZINES

H Texas Magazine: www.htexas.com
Houston: www.modernluxury.com

ON **THE** WEB

CultureMap: www.culturemap.com
Houston Tidbits: http://houston.gotidbits.com

APPENDIX C:

PUBLIC TRANSPORTATION

It's widely known that Houstonians love their cars, which is part of the reason that we're known for our insane traffic issues. If you want to take public transportation, however, you do have options that range from buses to light rail to Amtrak.

GETTING AROUND TOWN

METRO
(713) 635-4000
www.ridemetro.org

The METRO system includes more than 1,200 buses that service the greater Houston area. With Park & Ride facilities available to facilitate the rush-hour commute and dozens of diesel-hybrids in the fleet to ease the environmental impact, the system is working to address the needs of all types of Houstonians. Fares start at $1.25, although greater discounts are available. Check the website for routes and details.

METRO Rail
(713) 635-4000
www.ridemetro.org

It may not be the most user-friendly method of transportation ever created, but it's a good start for a city desperately in need of a functional rail system. Right now, the trains offer passengers convenient access to downtown, Midtown, the Museum District, and the Texas Medical Center, as well as connections that offer access to Bush Intercontinental Airport. Fares start at $1.25; discounts are available.

GETTING **OUT** OF **TOWN**

Heading out of Houston? Here are some options for affordable transportation.

Amtrak
902 Washington Ave.
(800) 872-7245
www.amtrak.com

Amtrak may not have the same reputation as the super trains of Europe and Asia, but if you're looking to head out of Houston, it's not a bad alternative to flying. The station is located just outside of downtown near the trendy Washington Avenue nightlife district, and the routes will get you to most areas of the United States. Amtrak is a particularly good option if you're heading out west, as there's a direct train from Houston to California. Check the website for station times and fare details.

Greyhound
2121 Main St.
(713) 759-6565
www.greyhound.com

Need to get to or from Houston? The Greyhound bus station, which is located in the heart of downtown, is open twenty-four hours and offers affordable transportation to cities across the country. Just be sure to arrive at the station early, as schedules may change.

Houston George Bush Intercontinental Airport
2800 N. Terminal Rd.
(281) 230-3100
www.fly2houston.com

One of the ten busiest airports in the United States featuring international flights that span the globe, Bush Intercontinental is an important part of Houston. And if you look carefully, you can easily find deals in and out of this airport, which is a hub for Continental Airlines and a stopover point for many others. For parking discounts, be sure to visit the Parking Cents value lot, where uncovered spaces are just $5 a day.

William P. Hobby Airport
16930 John F. Kennedy Blvd.
(281) 233-3000
www.fly2houston.com/hobbyHome

Looking for a bargain flying in or out of Houston? This airport is a good bet, as it offers flights on discount carriers such as Southwest Airlines, AirTran, JetBlue, and more. And, since it's smaller than Bush Intercontinental, it can be easier to navigate. Parking is more convenient, too.

APPENDIX D:

AREA LIBRARIES

HOUSTON PUBLIC LIBRARIES

Acres Homes Neighborhood Library, 8501 W. Montgomery Rd., (832) 393-1700

Bracewell Neighborhood Library, 9002 Kingspoint Dr., (832) 393-2580

Carnegie Neighborhood Library, 1050 Quitman St., (832) 393-1720

Central Library, 500 McKinney St., (832) 393-1313

Clayton Library Center for Genealogical Research, 5300 Caroline St., (832) 393-2600

Collier Regional Library, 6200 Pinemont Dr., (832) 393-1740

Dixon Neighborhood Library, 8002 Hirsch Rd., (832) 393-1760

Fifth Ward Neighborhood Library, 4014 Market St., (832) 393-1770

Flores Neighborhood Library, 110 N. Milby St., (832) 393-1780

Freed-Montrose Neighborhood Library, 4100 Montrose Blvd., (832) 393-1800

Heights Neighborhood Library, 1302 Heights Blvd., (832) 393-1810

Henington-Alief Regional Library, 7979 S. Kirkwood Rd., (832) 393-1820

Hillendahl Neighborhood Library, 2436 Gessner Rd., (832) 393-1940

HPL Express Discovery Green, 1500 McKinney St., (832) 393-1375

HPL Express Southwest, 6400 High Star Dr., (832) 393-2660

Johnson Neighborhood Library, 3517 Reed Rd., (832) 393-2550

Jungman Neighborhood Library, 5830 Westheimer Rd., (832) 393-1860

Kendall Neighborhood Library, 609 N. Eldridge Parkway, (832) 393-1880

Lakewood Neighborhood Library, 8815 Feland St., (832) 393-2530

Looscan Neighborhood Library, 2510 Willowick Rd., (832) 393-1900

Mancuso Neighborhood Library, 6767 Bellfort St., (832) 393-1920

McCrane-Kashmere Gardens Neighborhood Library, 5411 Pardee St., (832) 393-2450

McGovern-Stella Link Neighborhood Library, 7405 Stella Link Rd., (832) 393-2630

Melcher Neighborhood Library, 7200 Keller St., (832) 393-2480

Meyer Neighborhood Library, 5005 W. Bellfort St., (832) 393-1840

Moody Neighborhood Library, 9525 Irvington Blvd., (832) 393-1950

Morris Frank Library, 10103 Fondren Rd., Brays Oaks Towers Building, (832) 393-2410

Oak Forest Neighborhood Library, 1349 W. 43rd St., (832) 393-1960

Parent Resource Library— Children's Museum of Houston, 1500 Binz St., (713) 535-7264

Park Place Regional Library, 8145 Park Place, (832) 393-1970

Pleasantville Neighborhood Library, 1520 Gellhorn Dr., (832) 393-2330

Ring Neighborhood Library, 8835 Long Point Rd., (832) 393-2000

Robinson-Westchase Neighborhood Library, 3223 Wilcrest Dr., (832) 393-2011

Scenic Woods Regional Library, 10677 Homestead Rd., (832) 393-2030

Smith Neighborhood Library, 3624 Scott St., (832) 393-2050

Stanaker Neighborhood Library, 611 S. Sgt. Macario Garcia Dr., (832) 393-2080

Stimley-Blue Ridge Neighborhood Library, 7007 W. Fuqua St., (832) 393-2370

The African American Library at the Gregory School, 1300 Victor St., (832) 393-1440

Tuttle Neighborhood Library, 702 Kress St., (832) 393-2100

Vinson Neighborhood Library, 3810 W. Fuqua St., (832) 393-2120

Walter Neighborhood Library, 7660 Clarewood Dr., (832) 393-2500

Young Neighborhood Library, 5260 Griggs Rd., Palm Center, (832) 393-2140

HARRIS **COUNTY** PUBLIC **LIBRARIES**

Library Administration, 8080 El Rio St., (713) 749-9000

Aldine, 11331 Airline Dr., (281) 445-5560

Atascocita, 19520 Pinehurst Trails Dr., (281) 812-2162

Baldwin Boettcher at Mercer Park, 22248 Aldine Westfield Rd., (281) 821-1320

Barbara Bush at Cypress Creek,
6817 Cypresswood Dr.,
(281) 376-4610
Clear Lake City-County Freeman,
16616 Diana Lane, (281) 488-1906
Crosby, 135 Hare Rd.,
(281) 328-3535
Cy-Fair, 9191 Barker-Cypress Rd.,
(281) 290-3210
Fairbanks, 7122 N. Gessner Rd.,
(713) 466-4438
Galena Park, 1500 Keene St.,
(713) 450-0982
High Meadows, 4500 Aldine Mail
Route, (281) 590-1456
Jacinto City, 921 Akron St.,
(713) 673-3237
Katherine Tyra at Bear Creek,
16719 Clay Rd., (281) 550-0885
Katy, 5414 Franz Rd.,
(281) 391-3509
Kingwood, 4400 Bens View Lane,
(281) 360-6804

La Porte, 600 S. Broadway,
(281) 471-4022
Maud Marks, 1815 Westgreen Blvd.,
(281) 492-8592
North Channel, 15741 Wallisville
Rd., (281) 457-1631
Northwest, 11355 Regency Green
Dr., (281) 890-2665
Octavia Fields at Humble, 1503 S.
Houston Ave., (281) 446-3377
Parker Williams, 10851 Scarsdale
Blvd., Suite 510, (281) 484-2036
South Houston, 607 Avenue A,
(713) 941-2385
Spring Branch-Memorial, 930
Corbindale Rd., (713) 464-1633
Stratford, 509 Stratford St.,
(281) 426-3521
Tomball, 30555 Tomball Parkway,
(832) 559-4200
West University, 6108 Auden St.,
(713) 668-8273

CITY **PARKS**

The City of Houston Parks and Recreation Department was created in 1916 and now maintains 350 parks and more than 200 green spaces in Houston. Here's a list of the city's parks. For more information on all of these parks, visit www.houstontx.gov.

Agnes Moffitt Park,
10645 Hammerly Blvd.

Alabonson Park,
9650 N. Houston Rosslyn Rd.

Alief Community Park,
11903 Bellaire Blvd.

Allen's Landing,
1001 Commerce St.

Almeda Park,
14201 Almeda School Rd.

American Legion Park,
3621 Golf Dr.

Anderson Park,
5701 Beverly Hills Walk

Andover Park, 6301 Nunn St.

Antioch Park,
1400 Smith St./Clay Street

Apache-Elbert Triangle Park,
7000 Elbert St.

Aron Ledet Park, 6323 Antoine
Drive at Holly View Drive

Atwell Henry Triangle, 4000
Hirsch Rd./4200 Crane St.

Autry Park, 911 Shepherd Dr./
Allen Parkway

Baldwin Park, 1701 Elgin St.

Banyan-Camway Triangle, 7200
Camway St./6900 Banyan St.

Barbara Jordan Family Park, 2400
Wipprecht St./4700 Lee St.

Beech-White Park, 7551 Scott St.

Bell Park, 4790 Montrose Blvd.

Bendwood Park,
12700 Kimberley Lane

Beulah Maxie Park,
2625 Monticello Dr.

Beverly Hills Park,
10201 Kingspoint Rd.

Blackhawk Park, 9401 Fuqua St.

Blueridge Park, 5600 Court Rd.

Bonham Park,
8401 Braes Acres Rd.

Boone Road Park, 7700 Boone Rd.

Bordersville Park,
19622 Carver Rd.

Boyce-Dorian Park,
2000 Erastus St.

Braeburn Glen Park,
9510 S. Gessner Rd.

Braeswood Park, 2345 Maroneal
St./Kelving Street

Braeswood Parkway, Holcombe
Boulevard to South Gessner Road

Brentwood Park,
13220 Landmark St.

Brewster Park,
1790 Des Chaumes St.

Briarbend Park, 7926 Woodway Dr.

Briarmeadow Park,
7703 Richmond Ave.

Bricker Park, 4548 Bricker St.

Broadmoor-Kretschmar Park,
1500 Elliott St.

Brock Park and Golf Course,
8201 John Ralston Rd.

Brookline Park, 3300 Real St.

Buffalo Bayou/Tinsley Park,
18-3600 Allen Parkway/
Memorial Drive

Burnett Bayland Park,
6000 Chimney Rock Rd.

Burnett Street Park,
1500 Burnett St.

Busby Park, 6700 Hirsch Rd.

Cambridge Village Park,
13000 Nitida St.

Camp Logan Triangle,
6401 Coppage St./Rodrigo Street

Campbell Woods Park,
2315 Crestdale Dr.

Candlelight Park,
1520 Candlelight Lane

Canterbury Village Park,
12822 Northumb Rd.

Carter Park, 7000 Santa Fe Dr.

Castillo Park, 1200 Quitman St.

Catherine Adams Rawley Park,
4790 Rawley St.

Catherine Delce Park, 5700
Collingsworth St.

Charlton Park,
8200 Park Place Blvd.

Cherryhurst Park,
2120 Missouri St.

Chimney Rock Park,
11655 Chimney Rock Rd.

Clark Park, 9718 Clark Rd.

Clements Spaceway,
5100 Memorial Dr.

Cleveland Park,
200 Jackson Hill St.

Cliff Tuttle Park, 6200 Lyons Ave.

Clinton Park, 200 Mississippi St.

Cloverland Park, 3791 Hickok Lane

Cole Creek Park,
7200 Drowsy Pine Dr.

Cooper Road Park, 200 Cooper Rd.

Cottage Grove Park,
2100 Arabelle St.

Cravens Parkway, 5901 Main St.

Crestmont Park, 5100 Selinsky Rd.

Crooker/Moody Park,
400 Westmont Dr./West Canal

Croyden Gardens Park,
8400 Millicent St.

Cullen Park, 19008 Saums
Rd./18203 Groeschke Rd.

Cullen Sculpture Garden,
1000 Bissonnet St.

Cullinan Park, 6700 Long Dr.

Cullinan/Oyster Creek, Highway 6
South/Hull Airport

Curry Street Park, 7201 Curry Rd.

Cyrill Madison Park,
7401 Tierwester St.

Darien Park, 7100 Darien St.

De Zavala Park,
7520 Avenue J/907 76th St.

Delmonte Park, 3750 Del Monte Dr.

Diez Street Park, 4700 Diez St.

Dodson Lake Park,
9010 Dodson St.

Dow Elementary Park,
1919 Kane St.

Dow Park, 7942 Rockhill St.

Dylan Duncan Memorial Skate
Park, 3950 Rustic Woods Dr.

Earl Henderson Park,
4189 Elysian St.

East Tidwell Park,
9300 E. Tidwell Rd.

Eastwood Park,
5000 Harrisburg Blvd.

Edgewood Park, 5803 Bellfort St.

Edmonds Park, 6400 Hamblen Dr.

Eisenhower Park,
13500 Aqueduct Rd.

Elbert Park, 7400 Bayan St.

Eldridge Park, 2120 Eldridge Rd.

Ella Lee Park, 2030 Larchmont Rd.

Ervan Chew Park, 4502 Dunlavy St.

Elm Street Park, 7600 Elm St. at
Brays Bayou

Emancipation Park,
3018 Dowling St.

E. P Hill Park, 4790 Glory Land

E. R. and Ann Hobart Taylor Park,
1850 Reed Rd.

Evella Park, 5210 Evella St.

Fannin-Greenbriar Triangle, 7998
Fannin St./Greenbriar Street

Farnsworth Park, Basin Walden
Woods Subdivision

Finnigan Park, 4900 Providence St.

Fleming Park, 1901 Sunset Blvd.

Fonde Community Center,
110 Sabine St.

Fonde Park, 5500 Carrolton St.

Forest West Park,
5915 Golden Forest Dr.

Forum Park, 9900 block of Sugar
Branch Drive

Fox Park, 500 York St.

Francklow Park,1300 Seagler Rd.

Freed Art and Nature Park,
1400 White Oak Parkway

Freed Park, 7020 Shadyvilla Lane

Freeway Manor Park,
2241 Bronson St./2300 Theta St.

Freshmeadow Park,
4500 Campbell Rd.

Gail Reeves Park, 8790 Mullins Dr.

Garden Villas Park,
6720 Haywood Dr.

Garriott Tract, Belleau Woods

George T. Nelson Park,
3820 Yellowstone Blvd.

Gleason Park, 7200 Gleason Rd.

Glenbrook Park and Golf Course,
8201 N. Bayou Dr.

Glenmore Forest Park, 7900 Wingo
and Glemore Forest Street

Glenshire Park, 12100 Riceville
School Rd.

Godwin Park, 5101 Rutherglenn Dr.

Golfview Park, 6201 Cherryhill Ave.

Grady Park, 2120 Yorktown St.

Gragg Park Campus,
2999 S. Wayside Dr.

Graham Park, 540 W. 34th St.

Grand River Park,
8400 Grandriver Dr.

Greens Bayou Park,
700 Westmont Dr.
Greenwood Park, 602 Beresford St.
Gregg Street Park, 605 Gregg St.
Grimes Park, 5150 Reed Rd.
Groveland Terrace Park,
3921 Herald St.
Guadalupe Plaza, 2311 Runnels St.
Gus Wortham Park and Golf
Course, 311 S. Wayside Dr.
Hackberry Park,
7777 S. Dairy Ashford Rd.
Haden Park, 1404 Witte Rd.
Halbert Park, 200 E. 23rd St.
Hall Road Reserve, 9500 Hall Rd.
Halls Bayou Park,
7900 Tidwell Rd. at Halls Bayou
Harry Reed Park, 7500 Jensen Dr.
Hartman Park, 9311 Avenue P
Harwin Park, 11305 Harwin Dr.
Haviland Park, 11600 Haviland St.
Heights Boulevard Park,
Heights Boulevard (100–1900)
Hennessy Park, 1900 Lyons Ave.
Herman Brown Park,
400 Mercury Dr.
Hermann Park, 6001 Fannin St.
Hermann Square, 900 Smith St.
Hidalgo Park, 7000 Avenue Q
Highland Park, 3316 De Soto St.
Hirsch Road Park, 10790 Hirsch
Rd. at Little York Road
Hobart Taylor Park,
8100 Kenton St.
Hogg Bird Sanctuary Park, 100
Westcott St.
Hogg Park, 2211 South St.

Holly Anawaty Bark Park,
9100 Kingspoint Rd.
Homewood Park, 2943 Lazy Lane
Houston Gardens Park,
6901 Apache St.
Hutcheson Park,
5400 Lockwood Dr.
Independence Heights Park,
601 E. 35th St.
Ingrando Park, 7302 Keller St.
Irvington Park, 1000 Cavalcade St.
James W. Lee Park,
9025 Pitner Rd.
Japonica Park, 6600 Japonica St.
Jasper "Smokey" Frank Park,
13400 River Trail Dr.
Jaycee Park, 1300 Seamist Dr.
Jerry Sharp Park, 3234 Chaffin St.
Jones Plaza, 601 Louisiana St.
Joplin Street Park, 7401 Joplin St.
J. P White Park, 11891 Market St.
J. Robinson Sr. Park,
1422 Ledwicke St.
J. T Trotter Park,
7909 E. Little York Rd.
Karl Young Park,
7900 Stella Link Rd.
Keith-Wiess Park,
12300 Aldine Westfield Rd.
Kerr Park, 4620 Arlington St.
King Estates Park,
4791 E. Orem Dr.
Kingwood Park, 2700 Bens Branch
Dr. at Bens View Lane
Kirby Park, 900 Kirby Dr.
Knox Park, 229 S. Heights Blvd.
Lake Forest Park, 9200 Mesa Dr.

Lake Houston Park,
22031 Baptist Encampment Rd.
Lakewood Park, 8811 Feland St.
Lamar Park, 1400 Hyde Park Blvd./
Waugh Drive
Langwood Park, 3975 Bolin Rd.
Lansdale Park, 8201 Roos Rd.
Law Park, 6200 Scarlet Dr./
6100 Vassar St.
Lawrence Park, 725 Lawrence St.
Lee Hager Park,
12100 Landsdowne Dr.
Levy Park, 3791 Eastside St.
Ley Plaza Park, 1900 White Oak Dr.
Lincoln Park, 979 Grenshaw St.
Linear Park, Sabine Street
Linkwood Park, 3699 Norris Dr.
Little Thicket Park,
1831 W. 23rd St.
Live Oak Park, 2000 Brentwood Dr.
Love Park, 1000 W. 12th St.
MacGregor Park, 5225 Calhoun Rd.
MacGregor Parkway,
2200 MacGregor Way
MacGregor Way Park, 5791 Almeda
Rd./MacGregor Way
Magueritte Ray Park,
8401 Elrod St.
Mandell Park, 1500 Richmond Ave.
Mangum Manor Park,
5235 Saxon Dr.
Marian Park, 11000 S. Gessner Rd.
Market Square Park, 301 Milam St.
Mary Elliott Park,
3000 Chevy Chase Dr.
Mary Withers Park,
10600 Shady Lane

Mason Park,
541 S. 75th St./Tipps Street
Maxey Park, 601 Maxey Rd.
Mayfair Park, 6000 Arthington St.
McCullough Park, 901 E. 40th St.
M. C. Cullinan Park, 5120 Polk St.
McReynolds Park, 5905 Larimer St.
Meadowcreek Village Park,
5333 Berry Creek Dr.
Melrose Park, 1000 Canino Rd.
Memorial Park, 6501 Memorial Dr.
Memorial West Pocket Park,
13922 Memorial Dr.
Meyerland Park, 5151 Jason St.
Milby Park, 2001 Central St.
Milroy Park, 1205 Yale St.
Milton Park, 6150 Jensen Dr./
Caplin Street
Minola Park, 6415 Taggart St./
Minola Street
Mills Bennett Park, 3000 Ennis
St./North MacGregor Way
Moses Leroy Park, 3100 Trulley St.
Montie Beach Park,
915 Northwood St.
Moody Park, 3725 Fulton St.
Nacol Park, 4418 Bingle Rd.
Nellie Keyes Park, 791 Lester St.
Nob Hill Park,
10300 Timber Oak Dr.
North Houston Avenue Triangles,
3200 Houston Ave./North Freeway
Northline Park, 6902 Nordling Rd.
Nottingham Park,
14205 Kimberley Lane
Oak Forest Park, 2100 Judiway St.
Oak Meadow Park, 500 Ahrens St.

Old City Hall Clock Plaza,
Congress Street/Travis Street
Old N. MacGregor Spaceway,
1890 N. MacGregor Way
Olympia Park, 3600 Olympia Dr.
Our Park, 2604 Alabama St.
Park Drive Park, 4600 Park Dr.
Park Place Park, 8600 Detroit St.
Parkwood Park,
3400 N. Parkwood Dr.
Peggy Park, 4101 Almeda Rd.
Peggy's Point Plaza Park,
4240 Main St.
Pelham Park, 7500 Fountaine St.
Pershing Park, 5500 Pershing St./
Saint Lo Road
Pine Valley Park,
2431 Pine Valley Dr.
Pinewood Village Park,
2790 Briarwick Lane
Pleasanton Manor Park,
8501 Guinevere St.
Post Oak Park,
744 Post Oak Blvd./West Loop
Post Oak Village Park,
13790 Lockway Dr.
Proctor Plaza Park,
793 W. Temple St.
R. L. and Cora Johnson Park,
9801 Tanner Rd.
Randall P Jones, 1600 Summer St.
Rebecca Meyer Park, 3200 Reba Dr.
Reveille Park, 7700 Oak Vista St.
Richard T Brock Park,
2129 Bingham St.
River Oaks Park, 3600 Locke Lane
Riverside Park, 2600 S. Calumet
St./North Calumet Street

Root Memorial Square Park,
1400 Clay St.
Rosewood Park, 8200 Darien St.
Rosslyn Park, 6500 Pinemont Dr.
Sagemont Park, 11507 Hughes Rd.
Sam Houston Park, 1000 Bagby St.
Samuel Spaceway,
12936 Samuel Lane
San Felipe Park,
1717 Allen Parkway
San Jacinto Park,
22100 US 59/San Jacinto River
Sand Canyon Park,
13900 Sand Canyon Dr.
Santos and Esther Nieto Park,
500 Port St.
Scenic Woods Park,
7449 Lakewood Dr.
Schnur Park, 12227 Cullen Blvd.
Schwartz Park, 8203 Vogue Lane
Schweppe Park, 1791 El Paseo St.
Scottcrest Park,
10700 Rosehaven Dr.
Selena Quintanilla Perez Park,
Denver Harbor, 6402 Market St.
Sesquicentennial Park,
400 Texas Ave.
Settegast Park, 3001 Garrow St.
Shady Lane Park,
10100 Shady Lane
Sharpstown Green Park,
6300 Sharpview Dr.
Sharpstown Park and Golf Course,
8200 Bellaire Blvd.
Sheldon Park, 8815 Pineland Rd.
Shepherd Park, 4725 Brinkman St.
Simon Minchen Park,
4900 W. Fuqua St.

Sims Bayou Park, 9500 Martin
Luther King Blvd.
Siro Gutierrez Park,
7900 Flaxman St.
Sleepy Hollow Park,
3400 Sleepy Hollow Court
Songwood Park, 548 Westshire Dr.
South Main Estates Park,
12256 Zavalla Rd.
Southcrest Park,
5842 Southmund St.
Spotts Park, 401 S. Heights Blvd.
Spurlock Park, 6700 Park Lane
Squatty Lyons Park,
2121 Chamberlin St.
St. Lo Park, 7335 Saint Lo Rd.
Stewart Park, 6700 Reed Rd.
Stonecrest Parkway,
2701 E. T. C. Jester Blvd.
Strickland Park, 300 Highridge
Dr./Tammarack Drive
Stude Park, 1030 Stude St.
Studemont Spaceway,
790 Studemont St.
Stuebner-Airline Park,
9201 Veterans Memorial Blvd.
Sue Barnett–43rd Triangle,
750 43rd St.
Sunflower Park,
5000 Sunflower St.
Sunnyside Park, 3502 Bellfort St.
Swiney Park, 2812 Cline St.
Sylvan Rodriguez Park,
1201 Clear Lake Blvd.
Sylvester Turner Park,
2800 W. Little York St.
Tanglewilde Park,
9631 Windswept Lane

Tanglewood Park,
5791 Woodway Dr.
T. C Jester Parkway,
4201 W. T. C. Jester Blvd.
Tidwell Park, 9720 Spaulding St.
Timbergrove Manor Park,
1500 W. T. C. Jester Blvd.
Tony Marron Park, 808 N. York St.
Townwood Park,
3403 Simsbrook Dr.
Tranquillity Park, 400 Rusk St.
Trinity Gardens Park,
4903 Bennington St.
Tuffly Park, 3200 Russell St.
Uvalde Park, 1020 Uvalde Rd.
Vassar Spaceway, 1720 Vassar St.
Verde Forest Park,
8790 Brock Park Blvd.
Veterans Memorial Park,
1790 Tidwell Rd.
Victoria Gardens Park,
4900 Werner St.
Waldemar Park,
12120 Waldemar Dr.
Walter Jones Park,
7900 Coastway Lane
Walter J. Rasmus Sr. Park,
3721 Jeanetta St.
Wanita Triangle, 6600 Wanita Place
Warren Park, 4301 Topping St.
Watonga Parkway,
4100 Watonga Blvd.
West 11th Street Park,
2600 W. 11th St.
West End Park, 1418 Patterson St.
West Mount Houston Park,
10300 N. Houston Rosslyn Rd.

West Side Hike and Bike Trail,
Westpark Drive to Eldridge
Parkway
West Webster Street Park,
1501 W. Webster St.
Westbury Park,
5635 Willowbend Blvd.
Westchase Park,
9851 Pagewood Lane
Westwood Park, 4045 Lemac Dr.
White Oak Parkway,
1513 White Oak Blvd.
Wiess Park, 100 N. Post Oak Lane
Wildheather Park,
14900 White Heather Dr.
Wiley Park, 1414 Gillette St.
Williams Park, 15000 McConn St.
Willow Park, 10400 Cliffwood Dr.

Willow Waterhole Park,
5300 Gasmer Dr.
Wilson Memorial Park,
100 Gilpin St.
Windsor Village Park,
14441 Croquet St.
Winzer Park, 7300 Carver Rd./
Dolly Wright Avenue
Woodland Park, 212 Parkview St.
Woodruff Park, 8790 Woodruff St.
Wortham Center, 500 Smith St.
Wright-Bembry Park,
850 W. 23rd St.
Yvette Calloway Park,
6502 Allegheny St.
Zollie Scales Park, 3501 Corder St.
Zurrie M. Malone Park,
2901 Nettleton St./Anita Street

APPENDIX F:

HOUSTON PARKS & **RECREATION TRAILS**

Heading out for a run, bike, or walk? The Houston Parks and Recreation Department maintains nearly 115 miles of trails that are at your disposal. All are surfaced with either asphalt, concrete, crushed granite, or gravel and are multiuse unless otherwise indicated. For information about these and more, visit www.houstontx.gov.

Agnes Moffitt Park,
  10645 Hammerly Blvd.
Baldwin Park, 1701 Elgin St.
Bell Park, 4800 Montrose Blvd.
Bendwood Park,
  12700 Kimberley Lane
Beverly Hills Park,
  10201 Kingspoint Rd.
Blueridge Park, 5600 Court Rd.
Boone Road Park, 7700 Boone Rd.
Boyce-Dorian Park,
  2000 Erastus St.
Braeburn Glen Park,
  9510 Gessner Rd.
Brays Bayou, Gessner Road to Martin Luther King Boulevard
Brays Bayou,
  Lawndale to Forest Hill
Brays Bayou,
  75th Street to Evergreen Drive
Brentwood Park,
  13220 Landmark St.
Briarbend Park, 7926 Woodway Dr.
Briarmeadow Park,
  7703 Richmond Ave.
Brock Park, 8201 John Ralston Rd.
Buffalo Bayou, Bagby Street to
  Shepherd Drive

Burnett Bayland Park,
  6300 Chimney Rock Rd.
Cambridge Village, 1300 Nitida St.
Candlelight Park,
  1520 Candlelight Lane
Canterbury Park,
  12822 Northumb Rd.
Clark Park, 9718 Clark Rd.
Clear Lake Trail, Space Center to
  Bay Area Boulevard
Cleveland Park,
  200 Jackson Hill St.
Clinton Park, 200 Mississippi St.
Cloverland Park, 3801 Hickok Lane
Cole Creek, 7200 Drowsy Pine Dr.
Crain Park, 9051 Triola Lane
Cravens Parkway, 5901 Main St.
Crestmont Park, 5100 Selinsky Rd.
Cullen Park, 19008 Saums Rd.
Cullinan Park, 6700 Long Dr.
Delce, 5700 Collingsworth St.
Denver Harbor, 6402 Market St.
Dodson Lake Park, 9010 Dodson St.
Dow Park, 7942 Rockhill St.
Eastwood Park,
  5000 Harrisburg Blvd.
Edgewood Park, 5803 Bellfort St.
Ervan Chew Park, 4502 Dunlavy St.

Finnigan Park, 4900 Providence St.
Fonde Park, 5500 Carrolton St.
Forest West Park,
5915 Golden Forest Dr.
Forum Park, 9900 Sugar Branch Dr.
Franklow Park, 1300 Seagler Rd.
Freed Park, 6818 Shadyvilla Lane
Freeway Manor Park,
2241 Bronson St.
Freshmeadow Park,
4500 Campbell Rd.
Garden Villas Park,
6720 S. Haywood Dr.
Glenbrook Park, 8201 N. Bayou Dr.
Glenshire Park,
12100 Riceville School Rd.
Grady Park, 1700 Yorktown St.
Gulf Palms Park,
11901 Palmsprings Dr.
Hackberry Park,
7300 Dairy Ashford Rd.
Haden Park, 1404 Witte Rd.
Hager Park, 12100 Landsdowne Dr.
Halls Bayou, Little York Road to
Mierianne St.
Hartman Park, 9311 Avenue P
Harwin Park, 11305 Harwin Dr.
Haviland Park, 11600 Haviland St.
Heights Boulevard, 400–1800
Heights Blvd.
Hermann Park, 6001 Fannin St.
Herman Brown Park,
400 Mercury Dr.
Hill Park, 4800 Glory Land
Hobart Taylor Park,
8100 Kenton St.
Houston Gardens Park, 6901
Apache St.

Hunting Bayou,
I-610 to Lockwood Drive
Hunting Bayou,
US 59 to Cavalcade Street
Hutcheson Park, 5400 Lockwood Dr.
Independence Heights Park,
601 E. 35th St.
Ingrando Park, 7302 Keller St.
J. Robinson Sr. Park,
1422 Ledwicke St.
Karl Young Park,
7800 Stella Link Rd.
Keith-Weiss Park,
12300 Aldine Westfield Rd.
Kerr Park, 4620 Arlington St.
Lake Forest Park, 9200 Mesa Dr.
Lakewood Park, 8811 Feland St.
Langwood Park, 3975 Bolin Rd.
Lansdale Park, 8201 Roos Rd.
Law Park, 6100 Vassar Rd.
Ledet Park, 6300 Antoine Dr.
Lee Park, 9025 Pitner Rd.
Lincoln Park, 979 Grenshaw St.
Linkwood Park, 3699 Norris Dr.
Love Park, 1000 W. 12th St.
MacGregor Park, 5225 Calhoun Rd.
Mangum Manor Park,
5235 Saxon Dr.
Marian Park, 11100 S. Gessner Rd.
Marron Tony Park, 808 York St.
Mason Park, 541 75th St.
Memorial Park (with timing
track), 6501 Memorial Dr.
Montie Beach Park,
915 Northwood St.
Moody Park, 3725 Fulton St.
Nob Hill Park, 10300 Timber Oak Dr.
Northline Park, 6902 Nordling Rd.

Oak Meadow Park, 500 Ahrens St.
Old Katy Hike and Bike Trail,
  236 N. Dairy Ashford Rd.
Palm Center, 5400 Griggs Rd.
Pleasantville Area, 1400 block of
  Ledwicke Street
Reveille Park, 7700 Oak Vista St.
River Oaks Park, 3600 Locke Lane
R. L. and Cora Johnson Park,
  9801 Tanner Rd.
Rodriquez Sylvan Park,
  1201 Clear Lake Blvd.
Rosewood Park, 8200 Darien St.
Sagemont Park, 11507 Hughes Rd.
San Felipe Park,
  1717 Allen Parkway
South Main Estates Park,
  12256 Zavalla St.
Scenic Woods Park,
  7449 Lakewood Dr.
Schnur Park, 12227 Cullen Blvd.
Schwartz Park, 8203 Vogue Lane
Scottcrest Park,
  10700 Rosehaven Dr.
Shady Lane Park,
  10100 Shady Lane
Shepherd Park, 4725 Brinkman St.
Sims Bayou Park, Martin Luther
  King Boulevard to Scott Street
Sims Bayou Park, White Heather
  Drive to Townwood Park
Sims Bayou, South Post Oak Road
  to Croquet Lane
Songwood Park, 548 Westshire Dr.
Southcrest Park,
  5842 Southmund St.
Spotts Park, 401 Heights Blvd.

St. Lo Park, 7335 Saint Lo Rd.
Stewart Park, 6700 Reed Rd.
Stude Park, 1031 Stude St.
Sunnyside Park, 3502 Bellfort St.
Swiney Park, 2812 Cline St.
Sylvester Turner Park,
  2800 W. Little York St.
Tanglewood Park,
  5801 Woodway Dr.
T. C. Jester Parkway,
  34th to 43rd Streets
Timbergrove Manor Park and
  Trail, 1500 W. T. C. Jester Blvd.
Townwood Park,
  3403 Simsbrook Dr.
Tuffly Park, 3200 Russell St.
Verde Forest Park,
  8800 Brock Park Blvd.
Veterans Memorial Park,
  1800 Tidwell Rd.
Waldemar Park,
  11700 Waldemar Dr.
Westside Trail, Westpark Drive to
  Eldridge Parkway
Westwood Park, 4045 Lemac Dr.
White Oak Bayou, Houston Avenue
  to Studemont Street
White Oak Bayou, West 11th Street
  to Pinemont Dr.
Willow Park, 10400 Cliffwood Dr.
Wilson Memorial Park,
  100 Gilpin St.
Windsor Village Park,
  14441 Croquet St.
Yellowstone Park,
  3820 Yellowstone Blvd.
Zollie Scales Park, 3501 Corder St.

INDEX

Regional Travel at Its Best

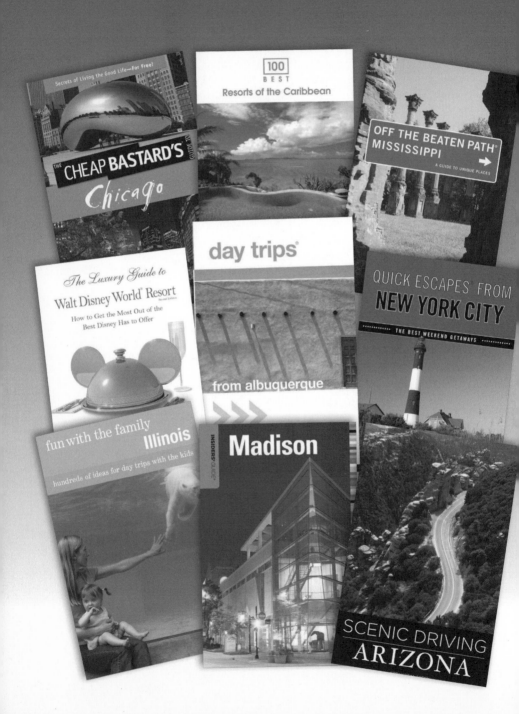